The Joy Of Christmas Collecting

by
Chris Kirk

Published by
L-W Book Sales
P.O. Box 69
Gas City, IN 46933

ISBN#0-89538-067-6

Layout and Design by:
Amy Van Hoosier

Table of Contents

Introduction 3
Pricing Note 3

Color

Figurines
Santa Claus 4-16
Reindeer 17
Miscellaneous 18-21, 97-98, 103

Ornaments
Elves 22
Musical Instruments 23
Angels 24
Clowns 25
Deer and Fish 26
Birds 27
Santa Claus 28-30
Buildings 31
Food 32
Pitchers 32
Miscellaneous 33-38, 93-96, 103, 109, 111

Light Bulbs 39-44, 101, 105, 109-113
Advertising 45-54
Calendars 55-58
Postcards 59-73
Trees and Wreaths 74-76, 93, 96, 101, 104-108, 114
Miscellaneous 77

Black and White

Advertising 78-83
Signs 84
Pails and Tins 85-89
Miscellaneous 90-92
Catalog Pages 93-114
Price Guide 115-119

Introduction

There are a few events that are as eagerly anticipated as the holiday of Christmas. An annual reunion of family and friends gathered together to share warm conversation, festive spirits, plenty of savory food, and generous gifts (IF you were good that year.) The Christmas season is quite apparent to us all, from the sparkle in a child's eye to the festive decorations that surround us all near the end of the year. Scenes of jolly fat men in red accompanied by flying reindeer. Blurs of green and red displayed around stockings full of toys. Towering evergreen trees adorned with glittering trinkets. Throughout the chilled evening air choruses of joyous carols delivered from huddled gatherings on front porch steps can be heard. The mouthwatering aroma of fresh baked goods mixed with the winter scent of chimney soot gently wafts beneath our noses. A nativity scene in the neighbor's front yard combined with the distant chime of church bells offers a subtle reminder of the cause for this celebration-the birthday of the Holy Son, Jesus Christ. All these examples are tell-tale signs that Christmas will soon be here.

Often the earliest sign of the approaching holiday season is when Mom retrieves the Christmas decorations out of storage. Glistening tree ornaments tucked carefully amongst a rainbow palette of ribbons and bows are brought out. Boxes of cheerful greeting cards are set aside in order to make room for the new ones to be received. Colorful figures of Santa and his elves see daylight once again after laying dormant for eleven months. Stockings are hung by the chimney with care as children scamper off to begin their "Christmas List."

Decorations have always been an integral part of the yuletide celebration. They become keepsakes generation after generation, passed down from loving mothers to their daughters. Also, as with any important aspect of the American life-style, they have become collectible.

THE JOY OF CHRISTMAS COLLECTING is a reference for those of us who love to discover remnants of Christmas past, continuing the search year-round. During your pursuit of adding these items and others to your collection, we would like to wish you happy hunting, have fun, oh, and most of all MERRY CHRISTMAS!

Pricing Note

Please Note! This is only a guide and L-W Book Sales cannot be responsible for any gains or losses incurred by the use of this book.

We have used an "average" in determining a price for all items. These prices will vary according to the region you live in.

Figurines
Santa Claus

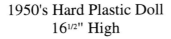

Papier-Mache
6¹⁄₂" High

1950's Hard Plastic Doll
16¹⁄₂" High

Metal Santas on Skis
2¹/₄" High

8" High

1940's Plastic Lighted
Santa Claus 17" High

Plastic Face - 12" High

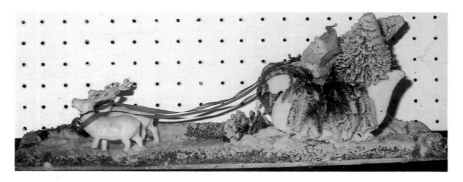

6" High - 20" Long

Early 1950's 4-6" High

Composition (from left to right)
Santa #1-5", #2-7", #3-6", #4-4"

Composition 16" High   Composition 19" High

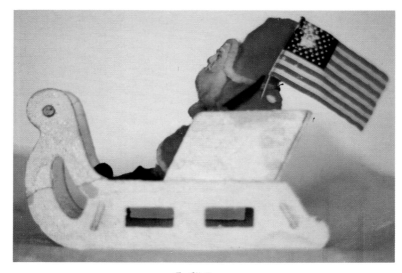

5-6" Long

Celluloid Santa 6" High

Celluloid Santas 3-6" High

Tin Mechanical Santa
Compositon
10" High

Battery Operated
Plastic 12" High

6¹⁄₂" Long

6" High

8" High

9" High

7" High

Composition
17" High

11" High
Pottery Body Parts

Composition
6" High

Composition
14" High

Straw Stuffed Santa
25" High

Composition
27" High

Both Occupied
Japan

Celluliod
6" Long

5-6" Long

Wood 6" High

Nodder 7" High

6¹ᐟ²" High

Bubble Light
7¹/⁴" High

Composition
10" High

13" High

Santa Figure
5" High

Ornament
3" High

Composition
7¹ᐟ²" High

1900's Papier-Mache
Santa 10¹ᐟ²" High

Papier-Mache Santa's
Large 9" High
Small 6" High

Reindeer

2-4" High

Celluloid
2-4" High

Miscellaneous

White Cotton
Left 4½" High
Right 3" High

Papier-Mache
Left 7" High Nodder
Right 5" High

14½" High

Hand Carved Santa Gnome
with Ashtray, Circa 1920

Light your yard with the joy of the

First Christmas

Tallest almost 2 feet

Similar to set at left except smaller, with unlighted sheep. C7½ bulbs not incl.
Mary, Joseph, Christ-child in crib.
71 N 98115—Wt. 6 lbs........Set $7.59
Shepherd and 2 Sheep.
71 N 98116—Wt. 4 lbs.......Set 4.59
3 Wise Men.
71 N 98117L—Wt. 6 lbs.....Set 10.29
Donkey and Ox.
71 N 98118—Wt. 4 lbs.......Set 6.59
Stained Wood Shelter. 22x30x16 inches.
71 N 98114L—Wt. 5 lbs.........$3.49

Beautiful Outdoor Nativity Set

Full-rounded figures of special molded plastic all
lighted from within .. tallest is 3 ft. high

Guaranteed 10 years $15⁴⁹ 4-piece set

Finished in weather-resistant paint. UL listed. 40-watt bulbs not included.
See Shipping Note below.
71 N 98124N—Mary, Joseph, Christ-child, crib. Wt. 14 lbs..Set $15.49
71 N 98125L—Shepherd, 2 sheep. Shpg. wt. 10 lbs............Set 10.79
71 N 98126N—3 Wise Men. Shpg. wt. 18 lbs.............Set 19.59
71 N 98127N—Donkey and Ox. Shpg. wt. 7 lbs............Set 10.49
71 N 98123N—Stained Wood Shelter. 22x47x37 in. Wt. 10 lbs... 4.49
Guarantee for plastic outdoor sets: If any figure breaks within 10 years
from date of purchase, due to defect in materials or workmanship, return
it and we will replace it free of charge.

Tallest 3 feet

Same as set at left, but in white. Mary,
Joseph, Christ-child in crib.
71 N 98119N—Wt. 14 lbs..Set $11.79
Shepherd and 2 Sheep.
71 N 98120L—Wt. 10 lbs..Set   8.79
3 Wise Men.
71 N 98121N—Wt. 18 lbs..Set 15.49
Donkey and Ox.
71 N 98122N—Wt. 7 lbs...Set   8.79
Stained Wood Shelter. 22x47x37 in.
71 N 98123N–Shpg. wt. 10 lbs.   4.49

Giant Decorative Garage-door Panel $5⁶⁹

Extra heavy weather-resistant fiber type paper. 103x77
inches. Mounting instructions included.
71 N 98206C—Shipping weight 5 pounds.........$5.69

Figures so real-looking you
expect them to move. Weather-resistant. Mounting stakes
incl. Shelter not incl.
16-piece Set. Wt. 59 lbs.
71 N 98204 N4–Set $68.95

Nearly life-size

2-dimensional figures
mounted on weather-
resistant hardboard—
tallest 4 ft.

Starter set $9⁹⁵   16-piece set $68⁹⁵

Mary, Joseph and Christ-child.
71 N 98200C—Shipping weight 9 pounds. .Set $9.95
3 Shepherds, Angel, 3 Sheep, Ox and Donkey.
71 N98201 N–Shipping weight 22 pounds. .Set $29.49
71 N98202N–3 Wise Men. Shpg. wt. 14 lbs. Set 17.49
71 N98203N–Camel only. Shpg. wt. 14 lbs.. 15.49

Shpg. Note: *"N" items (as 71N98119N) sent freight (rail or truck) or express.*   SEARS 393

1965 Catalog Page

Modern Cathedral

A new design for indoor nativity
sets with a backlighted
stained glass effect

$8⁷⁹

A truly beautiful set that shines with a simple
elegance. Inspiring cathedral background—a tapered triangle of rich dark wood frames stainedglass type window. Light in back casts warm
colors upon white semi-porcelain figures of Mary,
Joseph and Christ-child.

Mary figurine, kneeling, is 5 inches high; Joseph
6½ inches high and Christ-child 3 in. Set is 12½x
17¾ inches over-all. UL listed cord and bulb.
From Japan. Foliage not included.
71 N 97143—Shipping weight 3 lbs.... Set $8.79

Our finest indoor Nativity Set

Hand-painted figures look like wood carvings
.. distinguished by both size and beauty.
Tallest stands over 12 inches high

16-piece
lighted set $19⁴⁹

A skilled craftsman painstakingly chiseled into heavy steel to carve
the exquisite patterns for these papier-mâché figures. Then he filled
the precision molds. Finally he carefully hand painted the figures—
again and again to assure long-lasting quality.
Includes Mary, Joseph, Christ-child, 3 kings, angel, 3 sheep,
shepherd boy, donkey, ox and gold-color star. Wood-shelter 16x10x20
in. Plays carol from concealed music box. From Japan. UL listed.
C7½ bulb included.
71 N 97540L—Shipping weight 15 pounds............Set $19.49

Tallest figure $7⁸⁹
4¾ inches

Lighted 20-piece musical set. Elegant gold-color finish on papier-
mâché figures of Mary, Joseph,
Christ-child, 3 kings, angel, 2 shepherds, 5 sheep, donkey, camel. Wood
shelter 8½x11¾x4¼ in. UL listed
cord, plug, C7½ bulb. From Japan.
Shipping wt. 3 lbs. 4 oz.
71 N 97157............Set $7.89

Tallest $13⁶⁹
9 inches

15-piece unlighted musical set.
Includes papier-mâché figures
of Mary, Joseph, Christ-child,
3 kings, angel, 3 sheep, shepherd, donkey, cow. Wood shelter 18x7¾x12 inches. Concealed music box. From Japan.
Shpg. wt. 7 lbs. 4 oz.
71 N 97148.....Set $13.69

Tallest figure $5⁸⁹
4¾ inches

13-piece lighted musical set. UL
listed cord, plug, C7½ bulb. Mary,
Joseph, Christ-child, 2 sheep and shepherd. Papier-mâché figures from Italy.
71 N 97147—Wt. 5 lbs... Set $5.89
As above but no light, music.
Shipping wt. 4 lbs. 12 oz.
71 N 97146.............Set $4.19

1965 Catalog Page

Ornaments
Elves

Cloth Elf with Plastic Head
8" High

Cloth Elf with Plastic Head
8"High

Musical Instruments

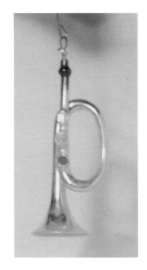

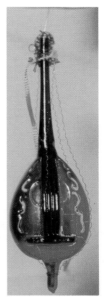

4-5" High

3-4" High

5-6" High

2 1/2" High

3 3/4" High

Angels

3-4" Long

3-4" High

6" x 3½"

3½-5" High

4-5" High

Clowns

Glass
2-3" High

4 ¹⁄₂" High

2-3" High

3-4" High

3-4" High

Deer and Fish

5-6" Long

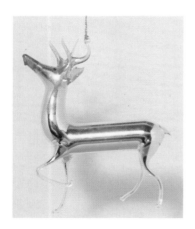

4-5" Long

5-6" Long

2-3" Long

Birds

4-5" Long

3-4" Long

4-5" Long

Santa Claus

3-4" High

2-3" High

2-3" High

2-3" High

2-3" High

Composition
2-3" High

3-4" High

3 x 9"

2 x 6" High

Chenille Bell 4" High

3¹/² x 1¹/²"

6 x 1¹/²"

2-3" High

Buildings

Church 3" High

House 3" High

Cardboard Building
2" x 3"

Food

Basket 2-3" High

Corn
2-3" High

Pear 3" High

Pitchers

2-3" High

2-3" High

2-3" High

Miscellaneous

Graf Zepplin
31/2" Long

All ornaments shown in this picture range
from 2¹ᐟ²" High to 6" High

2-3" High

4-5" High

3-4" High

2-3" High

34

2-3" High

3-4" High

4-5" High

Balloon Type
4-5" High

5-6" High

2-3" High

2-3" High

2-3" High

Gingerbread

Six men and 2 houses with icing that looks good enough to eat. About 4 in. high. Plastic. Hanging cords. Set of 8. Wt. 8 oz. From Japan.
71 N 93389.....Set 93c

Elegant Angels playing musical instruments

Gleaming gold color finished styrene. Each one plays a different instrument in this heavenly choir. Set of 8. From Hong Kong.
71 N 93248—2½ in. tall. Shipping weight 4 ounces..Set 93c

Gift Packages

To make your tree look gift laden. 4 square, 4 round. Made of shiny acetate with colorful ribbons. About 4x4 inches each. Set of 8. Wt. 4 oz.
71 N 93347......Set 93c

Smiling Faces

These jovial, happy heads made of decorated glass. Set of 3 includes Santa, Angel and Snowman. Hanging cords.
71 N 93276–Shpg. wt. 12 oz. Set $1.69

Striped Teardrops

White satin-finished glass with red, green, gold-color and blue stripes. Add a touch of holiday sparkle to any of your decorations. 8 in. long. Set of 4. Wt. 8 oz.
71 N 93269...Set $1.59

Hovering Butterflies

Hang on tree branches or to wreathes

5 in set 93c

5-inch long Styrofoam butterflies in assorted colors completely covered with metallic glitter.
71 N 93798—Wt. 8 oz..Set 93c

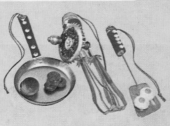

Mrs. Elf's Cooking Tools

Tiny spatula, frying pan and egg beater straight from the elves' kitchen. Decorated with simulated jewels and gold color flake. Set of 3.
Shipping weight 4 ounces.
71N93349–Set 93c

Metal foil Icicles

Resist flames. 20½ inches long. 1500 in package. Wt. 12 oz.
71N93043Pkg.79c

Metal Hooks

2½ in. long. For Scotch pine and flocked trees. 100 in package. Wt. 2 oz.
71N93612Pkg.23c

"Speedy drape" blankets your tree in love-liness

Loop attaches over treetop. Aluminum. 5 feet long. Shpg. wts. 3 oz., 2 oz.
300 silver color.
71 N 93630..53c
150 multi-color.
71 N 93631..53c

Top off your tree with a Golden Angel

Only 93c

11¾ inch gold color foil tree top ornament adds the perfect final touch to your holiday decorations. Wt. 6 oz.
71 N 93282...93c

SEARS 391

1965 Catalog Page

37

3-inch Figures in glass

Santa, snowman, angel and Nativity scene exquisitely detailed and set in glass. Hang on your tree or set on a flat surface. Box of 4.
71 N 93271—Wt. 12 oz. Box $1.89

Studded plastic Instruments

Add the perfect note of Christmas harmony to your tree. Each is 3 in. long, has cotton velvet hanging strap.
71 N 93348—Box of 3. Shipping weight 4 oz... Box $1.49

Velveteen Animals

Cotton. Handsomely made dog, donkey, squirrel and giraffe hang or stand. Christmas bows around necks. 5 in. long. Set of 4.
71 N 93297.....Set $1.98

Coffee and Tea Pots

Elegant hand blown 3-in. pots with handpainted gold color glitter. Satin white background. Set of 3. From West Germany. Wt. 9 oz.
71 N 93730....Set $2.49

Jewel-like 3-dimension ornaments

Crystal clear plastic surrounds sparkling figures and flowers

12 in Box $1⁹⁹

Whimsical figures peering out of delicately shaped ornaments add touches of delight to your tree. All about 4½ in. high. Wt. 12 oz.
71 N 93310........Box $1.99

Keepsakes

Six delicate glass ornaments, carefully hand blown and individually hand decorated. Produced from exact copies of original 60-year old molds. Wt. 8 oz. West Germany.
71 N 93800....Set $1.99

Handpainted

Satin white with glitter. 6-in. Peacock has plumed tail. 4½-in. Trumpet and Horn. Set of 3. Wt. 8 oz.
71 N 93470.Set $2.19

Elf-like Figures

Pine-cone dwarfs, Santas, angels, snowmen. Cotton felt. Stand on flat surface or hang from tree. Set of 15. Made in Japan.
71 N 93575-Wt. 12 oz.Set $1.39

Glass Ornaments

Carriage lamps, reflectors. Frosted, scenic, scroll or snowflake designs. About 2 to 2½ in. Set of 24.
71 N 93554-Wt. 11 oz. Set $1.79

Glass Teardrops

71 N 93622-Blue 71 N 93623-Red
Six, 4¾-in. Wt. 10 oz....Box 94c
71 N 93620-Blue 71 N 93621-Red
Five, 6-in. Wt. 10 oz......Box 94c

Pretend Candy Canes

Look good enough to eat. 7½ in. plastic. 6 in package. Shipping weight 4 ounces.
71 N 93379..........Pkg. 79c

1965 Catalog Page

38

Light Bulbs

Dick Tracy
2-3" High

Boy 3-4" High

Zepplin 3-4" Long

2" High

Milk Glass Bulb
2-2½" High

Milk Glass Bulb
2" High

Round Cone 3-4"

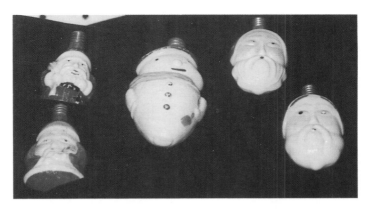

Decorated Milk Glass, All 2-2½" High
Except Snowman 3½" High

Lantern
2" High

8" High

Bell Lantern
2" High

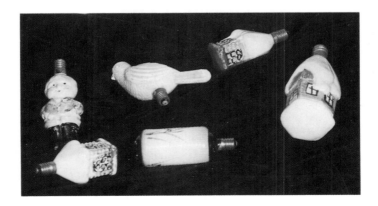

All 2-5" High

Milk Glass
2" High

Milk Glass
3-4" High

Flowers
3-4" High

1965 Hong Kong Mini Lamps

1965 Italian Imported Mini Lamps

Advertising
Miscellaneous

1960's Cardboard Santa
20" High

6' Cardboard
Stand-Up
Santa Claus
1960's

Paper Advertising
4¹/₂" High

Magazine 1912

14 x 18 Poster

1916 Magazine Cover

Easel Back 14"
Circa 1940's

Self-Framed
Circa 1930's
25 x 34

1950's - 48"

1964
6' Stand-up

1934

Ring Toss

Santa Advertising Ashtray
5¼" High

Coca-Cola 1970's Black Santa Stuffed Toy, 17" High

Coca-Cola 1970's White Santa Stuffed Toy, 17" High

Norman Rockwell Cardboard Santa
18" High

Coca-Cola Advertising
Plush Santa 1950's

Coca Cola Advertising

Plush Santa 1960's   Black Santa 1960's

1950's Cardboard Santa
20"

American Tissue Mills Cardboard
and Tissue Stand-Up
$19^{1/2}$ x $18^{3/4}$

Season's Greetings Cardboard 38 x 25"

Calendars

Postcards

#1 .... $3-5	#1 .... $4-6	#1 .... $4-6
#2 .... $4-6	#2 .... $4-6	#2 .... $4-6
#3 .... $3-5	#3 .... $3-5	#3 .... $4-6

Postcards

#1 .... $3-5	#1 Winsch $15-20	#1 .... $3-5
#2 .... $5-7	#2 .... $3-5	#2 .... $5-7
#3 .... $5-7	#3 Winsch $15-20	#3 .... $4-6

Postcards

#1 .... $4-6	#1 .... $4-6	#1 .... $3-5
#2 .... $4-6	#2 .... $4-6	#2 .... $4-6
#3 .... $3-5	#3 .... $10-12	#3 .... $4-6

Postcards

ALL CARDS ON THIS PAGE "HOLD TO LIGHT"
$25-35

Postcards

#1 .... $3-5
#2 .... $4-6
#3 .... $4-6

#1 .... $3-5
#2 .... $3-5
#3 .... $3-5

#1 .... $7-10
#2 .... $3-5
#3 .... $4-6

Postcards

ALL CARDS ON THIS PAGE ARE SILK
$25-30

Postcards

#1 .... $3-5   #1 .... $4-6   #1 .... $3-5
#2 .... $4-6   #2 .... $4-6   #2 .... $3-5
#3 .... $3-5   #3 .... $4-6   #3 .... $3-5

Postcards

#1 Clap Saddle $8-10
#2 .... $4-6
#3 .... $4-6
#4 Clap Saddle $8-10

#1 .... $4-6
#2 .... $4-6
#3 .... $3-5
#4 .... $4-6

Postcards

#1 Winsch $15-20

#2 Winsch $15-20

#3 .... $4-6

#4 .... $4-6

#1 .... $3-5

#2 Winsch $15-20

#3 .... $4-6

#4 .... $5-7

Postcards

ALL CARDS ON THIS PAGE ARE SILK
$25-30

Postcards

#1	....	$3-5	
#2	....	$5-7	
#3	....	$4-6	
#4	....	$4-6	

#1	....	$4-6	
#2	....	$5-7	
#3	....	$3-5	
#4	....	$4-6	

Postcards

#1	$5-7		#1	$5-7
#2	$4-6		#2	$5-7
#3	$5-7		#3	$5-7
#4	$3-5		#4	$5-7

Postcards

#1	$5-7	
#2	$5-7	
#3	$4-6	
#4	$3-5	

#1	$5-7	
#2	$5-7	
#3	$4-6	
#4	$5-7	

Postcards

#1	....	$5-7
#2	....	$4-6
#3	....	$3-5
#4	....	$4-7

#1	....	$4-6
#2	....	$5-7
#3	....	$5-7
#4	....	$3-5

Postcards

#1 .... $5-7	#1 .... $4-6	#1 .... $4-6
#2 .... $4-6	#2 .... $4-6	#2 .... $5-7
#3 .... $4-6	#3 .... $8-10	#3 .... $8-10

Trees and Wreaths

24" High

19" High

All 3¹/₂" High

16" High

#1-5¹/₂" High, #2-4¹/₂" High, #3-3-4" High

Miscellaneous

Compostion Wall Decoration
11 x 17

Plate 6" High

Advertising

Stuffed Snowman Figure
Circa 1970's - 20" High

Set of Four Stuffed Figures
Circa 1970 - 18" x 20"

Cardboard Easel Back
Circa 1940's - 14" High

Cardboard Easel Back
Circa 1960's - 18" High

Cardboard by Norman Rockwell
Circa 1960's - 19" High

Cardboard Easel Back
Circa 1960's - 4' High

Stuffed Snowman Figure
Circa 1970's - 20" High

Stuffed Mrs. Santa Figure
Circa 1970's - 18" High

Stuffed Caroller Figure
Circa 1970's - 30" High

Stuffed Elf Figure
1970's – 18" High

Stuffed Santa Figure
Circa 1970's - 20" High

Plastic 3-D by Norman Rockwell
Circa 1970's - 30" High

Cardboard Easel Back
1950's
18" High

Cardboard Easel Back
1960's
18" High

3-D Plastic/Cardboard
Circa 1950's- 24" x 28½"

Trolley Sign
Circa 1950's- 28" x 11"

Signs

American Tissue Mills
Cardboard & Tissue Stand-up
19½" x 18¾"

N.K. Fairbank & Co.
Paper 15" x 31"

Season's Greatings Cardboard
38" x 25"

Pails and Tins

Merry Christmas
(Jacob H. Stephens)
3¼" x 3¼"

Merry Christmas
From Santa
4½" x 2½" x 2¼"

Union Metallic
Cartridge Co.
57½" x 42¾"

Merry Christmas
(Little Chicago)
3¹/⁴" x 3¹/⁴"

Merry Christmas
(Londen Bros.)
3¹/⁴" x 3¹/⁴"

Merry Christmas-
Happy New Year
2¹/²" x 3"

Compliments of the Season
(C.G. Hogue)
3¹/⁴" x 3¹/⁴"

Merry Christmas
(Frank Fisher)
3¼" x 3¼"

Merry Christmas
(Hickory Street Church)
3¼" x 3¼"

Merry Christmas Heekin
Can Co. 3¼" x 31/4"

Merry Christmas (C.E.
Gunther) 3¼" x 3¼"

Brinkerhoff's 6" x 4" x 2"

Merry Christmas
(C.G. Hogue)
$3^{1/4}$" x $3^{1/4}$"

Night Before Christmas
$4^{1/2}$" x $2^{1/2}$" x $2^{1/4}$"

Compliments of the Season
3¹/⁴" x 3¹/⁴"

Merry Christmas
Happy New Year
3¹/⁴" x 3¹/⁴"

Merry Christmas
1898-1899
3¹/⁴" x 3¹/⁴"

Merry Christmas
(Ceto Finder)
3¹/⁴" x 3¹/⁴"

Miscellaneous

Santa Circa 1970's
48" High

3-D Plastic
Circa 1950's - 12" x 26"

Santa (Green Suit) on Reindeer
Circa 1970's - 48" High

A set of four
Postcards
meant to be
sent out one
at a time.

1915 Family Christmas Scene

EVERYTHING FOR THE XMAS TREE

CHRISTMAS TREE DECORATIONS.

These are the finest Christmas Tree Decorations it is possible to import from Germany and represent in every case exceptional value at the prices quoted. Carefully packed and exceptionally beautiful decorations for any tree.

One dozen beautifully colored fruit design glass Christmas Tree Decorations with attachment for hanging. Represent assorted fruits and show very plainly on the tree. Assorted colors and carefully packed. Size of box, 4½x6½ inches. Unmailable.

No. 8V6520 Price ....

Our 19-Cent Value.

Box of assorted beautiful design glass Christmas Tree Ornaments, including assorted color balls, fancy decorated designs, reflectors, and one fancy center piece. Large size and beautiful in assorted colors and designs. A handsome package for the price. Carefully packed in box.

No. 8V6521 Price ....
Unmailable.

Our Most Popular Box.

Beautiful Christmas Tree Decorations in assorted designs of glass balls. Assorted colors and designs with one large 10-inch fancy design glass Christmas tree top. Some of the ornaments are tinsel decorated, some have reflectors, some in plain colors and some beautifully decorated. Christmas tree top has fancy twisted effect stem and beautiful reflector mirror. A handsome box which would cost you 50 to 75 cents elsewhere. Each ornament carefully packed in cotton in box. Size of package, 8x13½ inches. Unmailable on account of glass.

No. 8V6522 Price ....

Our Finest Value.

The number of requests for an exceptionally high class package has caused us to put out this beautiful assortment. They are assorted designs, comprising silver Christmas bells, silver horns, angel boats, silver tinsel decorated balloons with basket, fancy shape balls, silver mirror reflectors and beautiful assorted colors of plain and decorated large size glass balls. Sells regularly for from 75 cents to $1.00. Twelve assorted designs, each carefully packed in cotton. This is the finest set we carry. Size of box, 9x13 inches. Unmailable.

No. 8V6523 Price ....

Christmas Tree Bead Decoration.

Ten long strings of ten large assorted color Beads. Large size beads in silver, pink, green and various assorted colors. Carefully packed in cotton in box.

No. 8V6525 Price
Unmailable.

Christmas Tree Top.

Fancy silver decorated glass Christmas Tree Top. Handsome in appearance. Four mirror reflectors and handsome shape tip. Length, 11½ inches. No tree is complete without this top. Carefully packed in cotton in box.

No. 8V6530 Price ....
Unmailable.

Silver Tinsel.

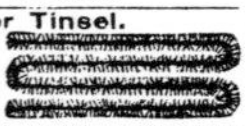

Six yards 1⅛-inch heavy fluffy Silver Tinsel for decorating the Christmas tree. You will be surprised at the added beauty that three or four boxes of this handsome tinsel will give to your tree.

No. 8V6570
If mail shipment, postage extra, 6 cents.

Santa Claus Snow.

Pure, white and sparkling. Used for Christmas trees and other holiday decorations. Merely sprinkled on the tree and floor gives that beautiful snowy appearance. Absolutely fireproof, superior to other preparations for this purpose. Put up in neat sealed packages. Shipping weight, 4 ounces.

No. 8V6572 Price, 2 boxes for....

CHRISTMAS TREE ASSORTMENT FOR ONLY

The Greatest Value for Decorating a Christmas Tree That Has Ever Been Offered.

Includes one box each of our Nos. 8V6520, 8V6521 and 8V6522 fancy Christmas Tree Ball Decorations, one tree top, five strings assorted color beads with ten beads on each string, three bunches of twenty each Christmas tree ornament fasteners, 18 yards beautiful heavy fluffy silver tinsel, two large packages tin foil tinsel, three Christmas tree candy stockings, two dozen assorted color Christmas tree candles, one dozen candle holders, large package Christmas snow, thirty fancy color and assorted design glass ball and picture tinsel decorated ornaments.

We have carefully studied this assortment and it represents to our best knowledge a complete and exceptionally high class assortment and sufficient for decorating a tree of average size. We urge you to buy this outfit and see for yourself how beautiful it is. Packed complete in box. Regular price, $5.00. Shipping weight, 5 pounds. This outfit only sold complete.

No. 8V6550

25-Branch Artificial Toy Christmas Tree.

Beautiful Green Branches, red berry decorated. This is for use on a table where a small tree is desired. Wooden base and five candle attachments. Width over all, 15 inches; height, 22 inches. Folds up completely for shipping and occupies little space. Shipping weight, 24 oz.

No. 8V6500

Christmas Tree Music Stand.

No Christmas tree is complete without a Music Stand. Plays two beautiful Christmas hymns and turns tree at the same time. Holds tree 1½ inches in diameter at base and tree is securely fastened by means of three screws. Has attachments so that music can be turned off any time and tree still turns. It amuses the children and makes Christmas much more enjoyable. Each music stand is nickel plated and packed complete in wooden box for shipment. Shipping weight, 8 pounds. Regular value, $7.50.

No. 8V6515

Jumping Santa Claus.

Miniature Santa Claus on spiral spring with dancing legs and arms, to be used for fastening on Christmas trees for decoration. Cloth cap, and beard in natural color. Regular price, 10 to 15 cents.

No. 8V6542

If mail shipment, postage extra, 24 cents.

Small Red Christmas Bells for Tree Decoration.

Height of Bell, 2¾ inches. Packed one dozen to envelope. Used for hanging on tree for decoration. Regular price, per dozen, 25 cents.

No. 8V6544 Our price, per dozen........
If mail shipment, postage extra, 3 cents.

Fancy Christmas Tree Candy Boxes.

Assortment of six fancy shape designs, as shown in illustration. Made of fancy color Christmas papers, crepe paper and fancy picture card decoration, with silver tinsel tops and handles. Well adapted for holding candy, popcorn, nuts and other Christmas delicacies. Very ornamental and very necessary on the Christmas tree. Each assortment in box. Shipping weight, 10 ounces. Sold only in box of six.

No. 8V6571

Santa Claus Masks.

This is the finest Mask we carry. Fancy oiled wax over cloth with heavy eyebrows, hair, mustache and whiskers. Heavy red felt hood with tie strings. This is an exceptionally fine mask and one on which there is little danger of breakage. Mouth is open showing teeth. Has dark lines under eyes, wrinkled forehead and other characteristics of the genuine Santa Claus face. Can be stored away and used year after year. It pays to buy the best. Length of face and beard, 13 inches. Regular $1.00 value. Packed in box. Shipping weight, 16 ounces.

No. 8V6505 Our price...........

Similar to the above, but made of heavy paper with heavy eyebrows, hair, mustache and whiskers. Has open mouth, wrinkled forehead and cloth hood. Carefully packed in box. Shipping weight, 14 ounces.

No. 8V6506 Price ....

Christmas Tree Candles.

Assorted colors. Good medium size and best quality. Packed in box. Shipping weight, 24 ounces.

No. 8V6581 Price, per box 24 candles.
No. 8V6582 Price, per box 36 smaller candles ....

Christmas Tree Candle Holders.

They pinch on the twig or branch and stay there. Can always be set upright no matter how twig hangs. Put up one dozen on string, one gross to box.

No. 8V6573 Price, per dozen......
If mail shipment, postage extra, 2 cents
No. 8V6574 Price, per gross......
Shipping weight, 30 ounces.

Christmas Tree Carpet.

This novelty solves the problem which has long vexed housewives every Christmas season. It affords protection to the carpet under the tree from wax and falling pieces of evergreen and at the same time is in keeping with all other decorations, adding to the charm and beauty of the tree. Printed on heavy muslin with fast inks, practically fireproof, with the design showing Santa Claus, reindeer, sleigh, house top, and holly border in natural colors, beautifully decorated. Can be washed and used year after year. Size, 60x72 inches. Shipping weight, 5 pounds.

No. 8V6595

Metal Christmas Tree Holder.

Every home will want one. Neat, convenient and will last a lifetime. Adjustable to a tree inches in diameter. Does not take up much space and sells at a price within the means of everyone. Can be fastened to the floor if so desired. When not in use can be folded up and put away. Width, 18 inches; height, 9 inches; weight 3½ pounds.

No. 8V6590

Christmas Stockings.

The Christmas stocking has come into universal use and is now regarded as indispensable in the holiday season. Beautiful design printed in five bright colors on very high grade muslin with indelible nonpoisonous inks. Made in the shape of a stocking. Merely sew the seams as indicated and you have an artistic stocking for filling with Christmas goodies, gifts and toys. Length, 16½ inches. Packed three stockings to package.

No. 8V6585
Price for three............
If mail shipment, postage extra, 2c.

Christmas Tree Stocking.

Small size for candies. Made of fancy lithographed heavy paper with small folding candy pocket at back. Front lithographed to represent real stocking and contents. Size, 3½ inches wide by 9½ inches long. Three stockings to envelope.

No. 8V6592
Price for three....
If mail shipment, postage extra, 2 cents.

1910 Catalog Page

Silver Tinsel Garlands

Smooth, well filled tinsel with fine cord in center.

78807   ¼ inch wide, ¼ gross yards in box.
78808   ¼ inch wide, ¼ gross yards in box.
78809   ½ inch wide, ¼ gross yards in box.
78810   1 inch wide, ¼ gross yards in box.
78811   1½ inch wide, ⅛ gross yards in box.

Tree Ornaments

COTTON SANTA CLAUS

Nos. 78800 to 78802   Nos. 78804 to 78806

78800   Cotton Santa Claus. Height 3 inches. 1 gross in box, not broken.
78801   Same as No. 78800. Height 3½ inches. ½ gross in box, not broken.
78802   Same as No. 78800. Height 6 inches. 3 dozen in box, not broken.
78804   Tinsel Christmas Trees. 2 inches long. Assorted colors in box. 3 dozen in box.
78805   Same as No. 78804. 3 inches long. 2 dozen in box.
78806   Same as No. 78804. 4 inches long. 1 dozen in box.

Santa Claus Snow—Fireproof

78821   Pure white and sparkling, just like the real thing, for decorating Christmas trees and other holiday decorations. Attractive sealed lithographed package.

Fibre Snow

78803   Fibrous Snow, a good substitute for snow. It clings to the branches of Christmas trees or other articles, producing a white snow effect, with the glitter of a real winter scene.

Christmas Tree Ornaments
We do not break packages

Christmas Trees

ARTIFICIAL CHRISTMAS TREES

Solid heavy wood pots painted white, limbs and branches are made of iron and covered with green foliage.

77613   Height 32 inches.
77614   Height 36 inches.
77615   Height 39 inches.
77616   Height 43 inches.

Tinsel Glass Tree Ornaments

No. 78812   No. 78813   No. 78814

Nos. 78815 and 16   No. 78817   No. 78818

78812   Three assorted designs. 6 dozen in box.
78813   Four assorted designs. 1 dozen in box.
78814   Three assorted designs. 1 dozen in box.
78815   Four assorted designs. 2 dozen in box.
78816   Six assorted designs. 1 dozen in box.
78817   Four assorted designs. 1 dozen in box.
78818   Assorted colored balls, with tinsel rings. 1 dozen in box.

Christmas Stockings

Nos. 77866 to 77870   Nos. 77110 and 77111

Christmas Stocking. Made of fancy colored netting, filled with assortment of toys.

77866   Length 10 inches. 1 dozen in package.
77867   Length 15 inches. ½ dozen in package.
77868   Length 18 inches. ½ dozen in package.
77869   Length 21 inches. ¼ dozen in package.
77870   Length 26 inches. Each in box.

Red Stocking. Removable Santa Claus head, has red cap, cotton hair, mustache and beard, sprig of artificial holly on side.

77110   Length 8 inches. 1 dozen in box.
77111   Length 11 inches. ½ dozen in box.

READY-TO-USE ELECTRIC DECORATIVE LIGHTING OUTFITS

In electrically lighted houses these ready-to-use outfits render possible most attractive effects and give an added charm to events and holiday celebrations. No flame, no dirt, no odor, no trouble, no danger. Complete with lamps, cord and socket. Ready to be attached to any electric light fixture in place of ordinary incandescent lamp. Has junction plug constructed in such manner that outfit can be increased or decreased by the use of extra festoons as desired. All outfits have extra lamps and are assorted colors.
The following is a list of the sizes supplied.
8 light outfit.
16 light outfit.
24 light outfit.
32 light outfit.

Candle Holders

No. 77902   No. 77904
                Per gro.

77902   Candle Holder with large round cup, string wire spring clasp with wire hooks upon which ornaments can be hung, finished in assorted colors. Measures 1¼ inches in length. Packed 12 dozen in box.
77904   Tack Candle Holder, showing half size. 1 gross in box.
77903   Ball Candle Holder, showing full size. ½ gross in box, all gilt.

No 77903

         Per gro. envelopes
78819   Contains 8 assorted Kringlettes, lithographed on both sides, strung, put up 8 in transparent envelope, 2 dozen envelopes in box.
78820   Contains 20 assorted Kringlettes, lithographed on both sides, strung, put up 20 in a transparent envelope. 12 envelopes in a box.

1917-1918 Catalog Page

Beautifully Colored Glass Ornaments

Our Finest Assortment. Our largest and most beautiful assortment consisting of 2 airships, 1 swan, 2 reflectors, 4 balls, and 3 Rugby shape, prettily colored. Trimmed with tinsel or frosted. Balls and reflectors are about 3 inches in diameter, swan and airships, about 7 inches high. Box 12x20 inches. Shipping wt., 2¾ lbs.
69F6515—Price, 12 for...........

A Pretty Assortment. Assortment of 12 fancy glass ornaments, average about 2¼ inches in diameter. Round, oblong and fancy basket shapes. All decorated in pretty colors. Shipping weight, 15 ounces.
69F6518
Price, 12 for.....

Assortment. This set consists of four reflectors, four oblong ornaments and four balls, all in bright colors, very nicely decorated with tinsel and frosting. Average size, 2 in. in diameter. Box 7½x10 inches. Shipping weight, 12 oz.
69F6521
Price, 12 for.....

An Inexpensive Assortment. This set consists of reflectors, balls and oblong ornaments. All in bright, assorted colors. Av. size, about 1½ inches. Box, 4½x6½ in. Shpg. wt., 9 oz.
69F6520
Price, 12 for.....

Asstd. Ornaments. A variety of shapes and colors. Some have painted decorations, some tinsel decorated. Reflectors, oblong and round. Av. size, about 1½ in. in diameter. Shipping weight, 1 pound.
69F6577
Price, 12 for.....

Assortment With Tree Top. This set consists of glass grape clusters, balls, reflectors, very nicely decorated in bright colors, also a fancy tree top, 8 inches high, other pieces about 1¾ inches in diameter. Box, 6¼x11 in. Shpg. wt., 10 oz.
69F6589
Price, 12 for......

Assortment. Contains 1 sail boat, 1 angel boat, and horn about 5⅝ in. long, 1 bird, 6½ inches long, including tail, 1 real tinkling bell, 4 balls, 1 oval shape, and 2 reflectors, beautifully colored and trimmed. The balls and reflectors are about 3 inches in diameter. Bell 3 inches long. Box, 12x14 inches. Shipping weight, 1⅞ pounds.
69F6509
Price, 12 for..........

Colored Glass Balls.

Beautiful glass balls. Rich, glowing, assorted colors. Twelve to box. Average shipping weight, 2 pounds.
69F6527—Diameter balls, 3¾ inches.
Price, 12 for.................
69F6510—Diameter balls, 3 inches.
Price, 12 for.................
69F6507—Diameter balls, 3 inches.
Price, 12 for.................
69F6505—Diameter balls, 2¼ inches.
Price, 12 for.................

12 Pretty Oblong Reflectors for

A fine assortment of glass oblong reflectors in assorted colors. The reflector part catches the light from the tree candles. Ornaments striped with bright green, red and blue colors. Average length, about 3¼ in. Packed twelve to box. Shipping weight, 1 lb.
69F6541
Price, 12 to box

Fruit and Vegetable Ornaments.

Made up of pressed cotton in shapes to resemble the different fruits and vegetables. Pretty natural colors, and some of them covered with sparkling mica. Size of pear, about 2¼ inches high; other pieces in proportion, assorted. Shpg. wt., 11 oz.
69F6581—Price, per box of 12.

Six Fancy Candy Baskets for

Guitar and Fancy Candy Baskets made of fancy colored Christmas papers, crepe paper and fancy picture decorations, with silver color tinsel trimmings. Guitar, 8 in. long. For holding candy and Christmas delicacies. Shipping weight, 10 ounces.
69F6571—Box of 6 for.......

Beautiful Glass Beads for Tree Decorations.

Strings of beautiful beads are very popular for hanging or draping over branches of the tree. Make a very pretty appearance and big display for small price. Carefully packed to prevent breakage. Ten assorted colored beads to string; 10 or 12 long strings (as described) to each box. Beads on string vary in size according to price.

Fancy Crimped ½-Inch Beads.
10 STRINGS FOR 59¢

Twelve 10-inch strings of fancy shaped beads to the box. Each string has ten beads about ½-inch in diameter in pretty assorted colors, with two small silver color beads alternating between the large ones. Packed in box. Shipping weight, 8 oz.
69F6527
Price, box of 12 strings for.....

11/16-Inch Round Beads, Assorted Colors.
10 STRINGS FOR 67¢

Strings about 11 inches long, consisting of ten 11/16-inch glass beads in assorted colors. Packed ten strings to box. Every tree should have a few strings of fancy colored beads to dress it up. Shipping weight, 10 oz.
69F6530
Price, box of 10 strings for.....

One-Inch Tinsel Covered Beads.
10 STRINGS FOR 139¢

Brilliant colorings. Ten strings about 13 in. long, consisting of ten beads about 1 in. in diameter trimmed with silver color wire. Some red and some green beads on each string. Shipping weight, 14 oz.
69F6540
Price, box of 10 strings for.....

9/16-In. Fluted Fancy Shaped Beads.
12 STRINGS FOR 79¢

A very attractive value in twelve strings of beads. Each string consists of ten fancy crimped 9/16-in. beads in assorted colors, with one small silver colored bead between the larger ones. Strings measure about 9 inches long. Shipping weight, 7 oz.
69F6538
Price, box of 12 strings for.....

¾-Inch Round Throated Beads.
12 STRINGS FOR 98¢

Each string is about 10½ inches long and consists of ten ¾-in. bright, attractive colored glass beads in assorted colors, red, gold and silver. Greatly improves the appearance of your tree. Shipping weight, 1 lb.
69F6529
Price, box of 12 strings for.....

½-In. Round Long Throated Beads.
10 STRINGS FOR 50¢

Ten strings of Glass Beads. Each bead is ½-inch in diameter. Ten large, assorted colored beads with small glass beads between. Strings measure abt. 12 in. long. Packed in box. Shipping weight, 1 lb.
69F6523
Price, box of 10 strings for.....

Novelty Pendant Strings.
12 STRINGS FOR 57¢

Twelve 6½-inch Glass Bead String Ornaments. Consists of 5 assorted colored ½-inch crimped beads with two small beads between each two of the larger and a 1¼-inch colored glass ball on the end. Shipping wt., 1 lb.
69F6546
Price, box of 12 strings for....

½-In. Round Beads With Small Beads Between.
12 STRINGS FOR 47¢

On a string about 9¼ in. are ten ½-inch diameter glass beads in assorted colors, with two small silver color beads between the large ones. Twelve strings to the box. Shipping wt., 8 oz.
69F6526
Price, box of 12 strings for....47¢

12 Birds for

Beautiful Glass Birds With Spun Glass Tails.

One of our prettiest and most popular ornaments. Fasten them on the branches of your tree with patent spring snap attached. They come in assorted colors and are packed twelve to the box. Each measures about 5½ inches in length over all. Shipping weight, 14 ounces.
69F6548—Price, per box of 12..

Beautiful Glass Bells.

Glass Bells, each measuring about 2½ inches high. Silvered inside surface. Swinging clapper makes tinkling sound. Assorted designs. Every tree should have a few glass bells on it. We sell them in sets of six and twelve. Shipping wt., 7 oz.
69F6514—Price, 6 bells.......59¢
69F6560—Price, 12 bells........

Six Pretty Waxed Angels.

Mohair wigs. Waxed finish. Glistening spun glass movable wings. Rubber strings for hanging. About 4 inches long. Shipping weight, 1 pound.
69F6516—Price, 6 for.......

Large Waxed Angel.

Movable glistening spun glass wings. Mohair wig. Length about 6½ in. Rubber string for hanging. Shipping weight, 2 ounces.
69F6517—Price, each.......

Unbreakable Ornaments.

Twelve brilliantly colored fireproof metal foil ornaments. Reflect bright colors. Can be kept from year to year. Average height, about 3 inches. Shipping weight, 1 pound.
69F6564—Price, 12 ornaments for ....

1921 Catalog Page

95

Ornament Assortments and Christmas Needs

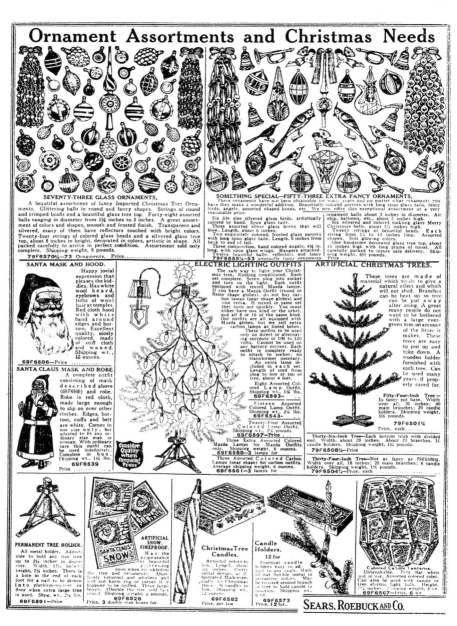

SEVENTY-THREE GLASS ORNAMENTS,

A beautiful assortment of fancy Imported Christmas Tree Ornaments. Glittering balls in round and fancy shapes. Strings of round and crimped beads and a beautiful glass tree top. Forty-eight assorted balls ranging in diameter from 1¼ inches to 2 inches. A great assortment of colors and shapes, smooth and frosted finish. Transparent and silvered, many of them have reflectors touched with bright colors. Twenty-four strings of colored glass beads and a silvered glass tree top, about 8 inches in height, decorated in colors, artistic in shape. All packed carefully to arrive in perfect condition. Assortment sold only complete. Shipping weight, 8 pounds.

79F6570¼—73 Ornaments. Price.......................

SOMETHING SPECIAL—FIFTY-THREE EXTRA FANCY ORNAMENTS,

These ornaments have not been obtainable for many years and no matter what ornaments you have they make a wonderful addition. Beautifully colored parrots with long spun glass tails, fancy birds, angels, assorted shaped horns, etc. We now offer this exceptional assortment at a very reasonable price.

Six life size silvered glass birds, artistically colored by hand. Spun glass tails.

Three assorted silver glass horns that will blow. Length, about 6 inches.

Two exquisitely colored, frosted glass parrots with long spun glass tails. Length, 9 inches from beak to end of tail.

Three composition, hand colored angels, 4¼ in. long, with spun glass wings. Hangers attached.

Twelve beautiful balls, reflectors and fancy ornament balls about 3 inches in diameter. Air ship, balloons, etc., about 7 inches high.

Six silvered and colored tinkling glass Merry Christmas bells, about 2¼ inches high.

Twenty strings of beautiful beads. Each string from 13 to 15 inches long. Assorted shapes. Soft glowing colors.

One handsome decorated glass tree top, about 10 inches high with long plume of tinsel. All carefully packed to insure safe delivery. Shipping weight, 6½ pounds.

79F6555¼—53 unusually fancy ornaments. Price....................

SANTA MASK AND HOOD.

Happy jovial expression that pleases the kiddies. Has white wool beard, eyebrows and tufts of wool hair at temples. Red cloth hood with white band around edges and bottom. Excellent quality, nicely colored, made of stiff cloth and waxed. Shipping wt., 12 ounces.

69F6506—Price ....

SANTA CLAUS MASK AND ROBE

A complete outfit consisting of mask described above (69F6506) and robe. Robe is red cloth, made large enough to slip on over other clothes. Edges, bottom, cuffs and belt are white. Comes in one size only, but adapted to fit any ordinary size man or woman. With ordinary care this outfit can be used indefinitely. Complete in box. Shipping wt., 1¼ lbs.

69F6539

Price ....

ELECTRIC LIGHTING OUTFITS

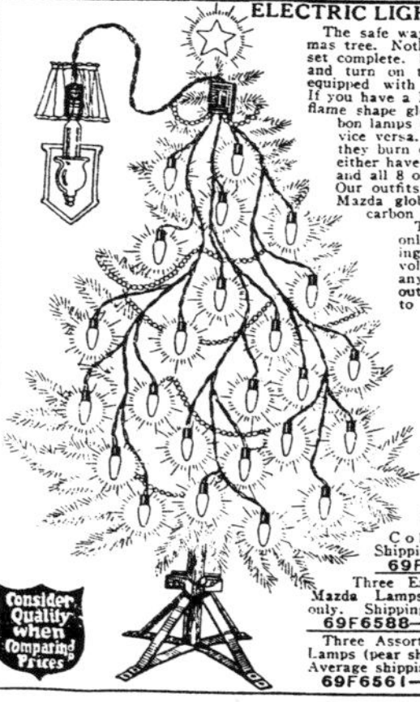

The safe way to light your Christmas tree. Nothing complicated. Each set complete. Screw plug into socket and turn on the light. Each outfit equipped with tested Mazda lamps. If you have a Mazda Outfit (round or flame shape globes), do not buy carbon lamps (pear shape globes) and vice versa. If mixed in same set they burn out quickly. You must either have one kind or the other, and all 8 or 16 of the same kind. Our outfits are all equipped with Mazda globes, but we sell extra carbon lamps as listed below.

These outfits to be used only on direct or alternating currents of 100 to 120 volts. Cannot be used on any battery current. Each outfit is complete ready to attach to socket; no transformer necesary.

An extra lamp included in each set. Length of cord from plug to box at top of tree, about 4 feet.

Eight Assorted Colored Lamp Outfit. Shipping wt., 1¼ lbs.

69F6593—

Sixteen Assorted Colored Lamp Outfit. Shipping wt., 2¼ lbs.

69F6543—

Twenty-Four Assorted Colored Lamp Outfit. Shipping wt., 3¼ pounds.

69F6597—Price .

Three Extra Assorted Colored Mazda Lamps for Mazda Outfits only. Shipping weight, 6 ounces.

69F6588—3 lamps for. ...

Three Assorted Colored Carbon Lamps (pear shape) for carbon outfits. Average shipping weight, 6 ounces.

69F6561—3 lamps for......

ARTIFICIAL CHRISTMAS TREES.

These trees are made of material which tends to give a natural effect and which will not shed. Branches can be bent up so tree can be put away after using. A great many people do not want to be bothered with a large evergreen tree on account of the litter it makes. These trees are easy to put up and take down. A wooden holder furnished with each tree. Can be used many years if properly cared for.

Fifty-Four-Inch Tree—In fancy pot base. Width over all, 30 inches; 40 main branches; 20 candle holders. Shipping weight, 5½ pounds.

79F6501¼

Price, each........

Thirty-Six-Inch Tree—Each bottom limb with divided end. Width, about 20 inches. About 23 branches, 10 candle holders. Shipping weight, 1¾ pounds.

79F6508¼—Price ....

Thirty-Four-Inch Tree—Not as fancy as 79F6508¼. Width over all, 18 inches; 20 main branches; 6 candle holders. Shipping weight, 1½ pounds.

79F6504¼—Price, each ....

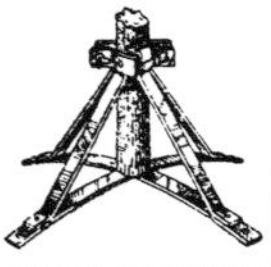

PERMANENT TREE HOLDER.

All metal holder. Adjustable to hold any size tree up to 2½ inches in diameter. Width, 15½ inches; height, 7¼ inches. There is a hole in the end of each foot for a nail to be driven into platform-support or floor when extra large tree is used. Shpg. wt., 2¼ lbs.

69F6591—Price

ARTIFICIAL SNOW. FIREPROOF.

Has the appearance of beautiful glistening snow when sprinkled on the tree and ornaments. Absolutely fireproof and odorless and will not harm rug or carpet if it happens to be spilled. Three large boxes. (Double the size sold last year.) Shipping weight, 2 pounds.

69F6528

Price, 3 double size boxes for.

Christmas Tree Candles.

Assorted colors to box. Length, about 5¼ inches. Pretty spiral design, as illustrated. Made especially for Christmas trees. 36 candles to box. Shipping wt., 12 ounces.

69F6582

Price, per box

Candle Holders.

12 for

Practical candle holders easy to adjust to any angle. Made of flat flexible metal in attractive colors. May be twisted around branch of tree to hold candle in position. Shipping wt., 6 oz.

69F6573

Price, 12 for..

Colored Candle Lanterns.

Unbreakable. Fold flat when not in use. Assorted colored sides. Can also be used with candle or tree electric light bulb. Height, 2¼ inches. Shipping weight, 8 oz.

69F6567—Price, 6 for.

SEARS, ROEBUCK AND CO.

1921 Catalog Page

CHRISTMAS NOVELTIES (Continued)

China Face Santa Claus Figures, with Beautifully Colored Cotton and Crepe Paper Suit and Hat. Our Own Exclusive Importation

60/1037

6005

6025	Santa Claus Figure Sitting on Square Box, 4½ inches............................
6023	Santa Claus Figure with Paper Basket on Back, 7 inches......................
6026	Santa Claus Figure Sitting on Tree Stump and Logs, Assorted, 7 in..
6005	Santa Claus Figure, Standing Position Box, 7½ inches.......................
6011	Santa Claus Figure, Standing Position Box, 9½ inches.......................
6024	Santa Claus Figure, Standing Position with Basket Container on Back, 9½ inches. ....
6028	Santa Claus Figure Sitting on Tree Log and Stump, Assorted (Box), 10½ inches. ....
6030	Large Santa Claus Figure Sitting on Tree Stump and Log, Assorted (Box), 21 inches. ....
6036	Santa Claus Figure Sitting on White Wood Sled with Nicely Decorated Sack Container, 6½ inches...............................
6037	Same as 6036 but size, 9¼ inches...............................
6038	Same as 6036 but size, 10¼ inches...............................
60/1037	Santa Claus with Red Cloth Coat, Pulling Open Wooden Sled, Mounted on Frosted Wood Base, 17 inches......................
10912	Santa Claus with Red Cloth Coat Pulling Open Wood Sled, Mounted on Polished Wood Base, 15 inches...............................
10913	Same as 10912 but size, 20 inches...............................

RED COTTON SANTA CLAUS FIGURES

520/106	Red Cotton Santa Claus, 2¼ inches...............................
520/107	Red Cotton Santa Claus, 4 inches...............................
520/108	Red Cotton Santa Claus, 6 inches...............................
520/109	Red Cotton Santa Claus on Snowball, 3 inches...............................
355/540	Red Cotton Santa Claus Figure (Box), 8½ inches...............................
60/1035	Jointed Santa Claus with Red Cloth Coat and Blue Cloth Trousers, 8 inches. ....
60/1036	Jointed Santa Claus with Red Cloth Coat and Blue Cloth Trousers, 11 inches. ....

CELLULOID SANTA CLAUS FIGURES

Well made of heavy celluloid and beautifully colored.

35/151	Celluloid Santa Claus Figure with Bag of Toys, 4¼ inches......................
35/152	Celluloid Santa Claus Figure with Bag of Toys, 5¾ inches......................
35/153	Celluloid Santa Claus Figure with Bag of Toys, 7½ inches......................
35/154	Celluloid Santa Claus Figure with Bag of Toys, 9½ inches......................

1925 Catalog Page

CHRISTMAS NOVELTIES

1289/8

10812

4015	Red Coat Santa Claus with Tree, 4 inches..
4016	Red Coat Santa Claus with Tree, 6½ inches...
4017	Red Coat Santa Claus with Basket on Back, 4½ inches.............................
4018	Red Coat Santa Claus with Basket on Back, 7 inches...............................
4019	Red Coat Santa Claus with Basket on Back, 9 inches...............................
4020	Red Coat Santa Claus with White Fur Trimming and Tree, 9½ inches.
4021	Red Coat Santa Claus with White Fur Trimming and Tree, 10½ in.....
18774	Red Paper Mache Santa Claus, 3 inches..
34420	Red Paper Mache Santa Claus with Shaking Head, 3¼ inches.............
9816	Red Paper Mache Santa Claus Box, 4½ inches..
9713	Red Painted Santa Claus Box, 5 inches..
9823	Painted Santa Claus Figure on Wire Spring, 2 inches.............................
9824	Painted Santa Claus Figure with Shaking Head on Box, 3¾ inches.....
24803	Painted Santa Claus Figure on Round Box, 3½ inches............................
24804	Painted Santa Claus Figure on Round Box, 4½ inches............................
1289	Painted Santa Claus Figure on Glistening Snowball, Box, 4 inches......

SANTA CLAUS FIGURES WITH PAINTED BLUE TROUSERS AND WHITE FUR BEARD

1289/7	Santa Claus (Box), 7 inches...
1289/8	Santa Claus (Box), 8 inches...
1289/9	Santa Claus (Box), 10 inches...
1289/10	Santa Claus (Box), 12 inches...

SANTA CLAUS FIGURES WITH BLUE CLOTH TROUSERS AND WHITE FUR BEARD

1289/11	Santa Claus (Box), 8 inches...
1289/12	Santa Claus (Box), 9 inches...
1289/13	Santa Claus (Box), 10 inches...
1289/14	Santa Claus (Box), 12 inches...
1289/15	Santa Claus (Box), 14 inches...
1289/16	Santa Claus (Box), 18 inches...
1289/17	Santa Claus (Box), 26 inches...

SANTA CLAUS FIGURES WITH BLUE CLOTH TROUSERS AND WHITE FUR BEARD, STOOPING POSITION CARRYING SACK ON BACK

10812	Santa Claus, 8 inches..
10813	Santa Claus, 9½ inches...
10814	Santa Claus, 14 inches..

SANTA CLAUS FIGURE WITH MECHANICAL MUSIC BOX

1289/21 Santa Claus Figure, Box, with Long Red Coat, White Fur Beard. Has Mechanical Music Box which Plays Christmas Carols, 22 inches. ....

1925 Catalog Page

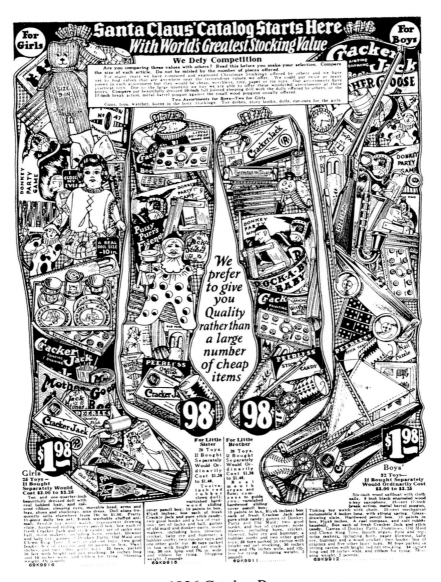

1926 Catalog Page

Prize Stocking for Christmas

The Greatest Toy Bargain in Our 55 Years!

Packed-Crammed-Jammed With Santa's Choicest Gifts for Boys and Girls

Boys! Big Surprise Package FREE With This Stocking

Girls! Big Surprise Package FREE With This Stocking

and a Big Surprise Package, Too!

Bigger and Better Than Ever Before

Never before have we seen such big Christmas Stockings like these, so brimful of quality toys, offered for less than $2.50 each—in fact they are far superior to those usually sold even at that price. The toys are real, not simply "fillers." They are just the bona-fide toys about which boys and girls write to Santa Claus and just the thing, too, for the teacher who needs an assortment of individual presents for the kiddies.

Free Surprise Package With Each Stocking

Even without considering the Surprise Package, this is the best Christmas Stocking value ever offered. We won't tell you how much this toy is worth, as it is our Christmas gift to your little boy or girl; but we know that this surprise package will complete your satisfaction to overflowing. To convince those parents who have never as yet become familiar with this yearly holiday offer, we are selling the stocking on approval. If you find that they do not give you more for your money, return the stockings to us and we will refund what you have paid, including transportation charges both ways.

33 Select Toys 33

For Boys
Feature Toys

1. A. C. Gilbert's well known size 4 58c Erector Set.
2. Complete printing outfit. Rubber type stamp pad and holder.
3. All the parts for making a windmill of galvanized steel, 14¾ inches high.
4. An eleven-inch airplane, of wood, that will actually fly.
5. Dandy, genuine leather covered baseball, made by well known manufacturer.
6. Break action, cork shooting pop gun, 14 inches long.
7. Filmoscope with 20 films.
8. Brass-lined telescope.
9. Magnetic compass with glass face.

and 24 Other Useful Toys

For Girls
Feature Toys

1. A Meteor Mosaic game, in handsomely lithographed box. Makes unlimited number of designs. Value 59c.
2. A 5½-foot jumping rope.
3. Embroidery set with wooden hoops, doilies, colored mercerized embroidery cotton and a needle. Complete with 20 pictures—a show in itself.
4. Imitation Leather Purse.
5. Bisque Baby Doll.
6. Real Scissors—and good ones.
7. Necklace.
8. Package of Stencils.

and 24 Other Toys the Girl Will Like

Don't Forget!
A Surprise Package Included With Each Stocking

You Can't Equal the Value Elsewhere for Less Than $2.50

The Boy Will Enjoy Every One of These Toys
Mother Could Not Select a Better Assortment

There are hours of fun in store for him with the A. C. Gilbert Real Erector set. The complete rubber type Printing Outfit enables him to print his own cards or toy circus programs. Windmill parts for assembling, all ready to put together with necessary nuts and bolts. An 11-inch airplane of wood that will actually fly. A Magnetic Compass to take on those long hikes to show the way. A baseball, break action popgun, and Filmoscope with films—are also fun makers for all.

There is a nickel-plated flute that may be played like a real instrument; a horse shoe magnet that will always be a novelty; a nail puzzle that amuses all; a frog snapper that "clicks" when pressed between the fingers; an imported horn, 10 inches long, guaranteed to make a lot of noise. He can play grown-up with the make-believe spectacles and have his friends put their finger in the end of the finger trap and they can't get away until he loosens it. Lithographed metal globe on stand shows practically all the countries, oceans and rivers in colors, a real help for geography lessons. Whistling tickler uncurls when he blows into the wooden mouthpiece. It's loads of fun painting with the water

colors, and he can surprise everyone by making pictures appear in the ten-page magic book—just brush clear water over the invisible colors, and presto, beautifully colored pictures appear. Story book printed in colors on good paper. A dandy wood top and string; a wooden noise maker; spinning flyer that rises high into the air.

He can imitate the movie comedians with the tiny imitation straw hat with elastic to go under the chin. Also a Chinese puzzle that never grows old; full size polleman's star to pin on his coat when playing copper with the other boys; box of eight imported stencils; pocket magnifying glass; with folding handle, may be carried in the pocket and used as a burning glass; toy rake, spade and scoop copied after those used by sea captains. Every toy a real, substantial plaything particularly suited to boys. And don't forget the FREE SURPRISE PACKAGE. How delightfully surprised he will be with it—for it is Ward's Christmas Gift to the boy.

Shipping weight, 6 pounds.

448 G 5557—Complete

Many Hours Amusement for the Little Girl
She Will Enjoy These Long After Christmas

All the toys listed above—and many others are contained in this dandy stocking for the little girl. Hours of interesting and fascinating fun with the bright blue, red, yellow and green marbles of the Meteor Mosaic game. The girl can make hundreds of interesting designs with it—each one new and beautiful. A 5½-foot jumping rope with wooden handles. A clever little embroidery set with 3 white cotton beachcloth doilies, hoops and skeins of colored thread and needle! She can entertain all her little girl friends with the Filmoscope and 20 pictures, a show in itself. A story book, printed in colors on good paper. A pair of safe, round pointed sharp cutting-out scissors.

A roll of assorted colored kindergarten paper for "cutting out"; the famous game of "Old Maid"—a set of colored cardboard dolls with paper clothing in which to dress them; a brightly colored bead necklace just like mother's; polished metal flute; aluminum knife, fork and spoon set; imported Japanese fan, with 14 white wood ribs. Large wool bowl bubble pipe; real red leatherette purse that may be used when mother sends her to the store. Pair of adjustable play spectacles; eight imported stencils;

a mirror and stand. Small bisque baby doll with jointed arms and legs; lots of fun painting with water colors and brush all in a metal box. Aerial spinner flies high into the air. 10-inch horn with wood mouthpiece frog snapper. Kdu-tional lithographed globe shows practically all oceans, rivers and countries in colors; a finger tickler—put your finger in the end and try to get it out. Ten-page book with invisible pictures, brush little clear water and beautifully colored pictures appear. Miniature imitation straw hat with elastic to put under the chin. Wooden noise maker that buzzes when she twirls it around. A garden rake, hoe and spade are all "fun makers" too. It totals thirty-three selected toys, and besides will receive a FREE SURPRISE PACKAGE, Ward's Christmas gift for the girl. It will be amazing value—the GUARANTEE. We believe every little girl will find one of these stockings her on Christmas morning—it will make this "c of days" more complete. Shipping weight, pounds.

448 G 5568—Complete

1928 Catalog Page

100

CHRISTMAS TREE LIGHTING OUTFITS

Fancy Lamps

An eight light fancy lamp outfit with flush extender and parallel lead.

No. 420 Fancy German Lamp Outfit ..

One outfit in a box

FANCY COLORED MAZDA LAMPS

For Christmas Tree Outfits

Lemons	box of 10,
Peaches	box of 10,
Oranges	box of 10,
Pears	box of 10,
Pumpkins	box of 10,
Birds	box of 10,
Monkeys	box of 10,
Owls	box of 10,

Ten in a box

PLAIN COLORED MAZDA LAMPS

For Christmas Tree Outfits

Green	each,
Orange	each,
Blue	each,
White	each,
Red	each,

Ten in a box

CHRISTMAS TREE HOLDER

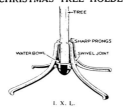

I. X. L.

By placing base of tree firmly in water bowl, the sharp prongs are automatically brought against the tree and hold it erect.

I. X. L. Christmas Tree Holder
One in a box

CHRISTMAS WREATHS

NOMA

A 12 in. Christmas wreath made on full round frame covered with red wood chenille roping. The decoration at the bottom of the candle consists of natural pine branches, chemically prepared, and holly leaves with berries, centered by a silvered poinsetta. The candle shaft is sprayed in silver and green with dript effect. Equipped with intermediate candelabra base Mazda Tungsten lamp, for 110-120 volts.

No. 1000 Christmas Wreath

One in a box

AUTO CHRISTMAS WREATHS

NOMA

A 6 in. wreath made of silk chenille with a 6 volt Mazda lamp, set in an attractive candle. The silk wire lead from the wreath is finished with auto lamp bayonet type base, for single or double contact, as desired. For 6 volt storage battery.

No. 1500 Auto Wreath

One in a box

Our building is equipped for speed and efficiency.

1928 Catalog Page

Musical
Roly Poly

Tip Santa Claus and you'll hear the pretty Christmas chimes. Fat, jolly, roly-poly Santa has real white fur whiskers and a red and white felt suit. It's lots of fun for baby to see Santa roll around for no matter how hard he pats him, Santa will always bob up smiling. Made of good quality papier mache. Height, 10¼ inches; width, 5½ inches. Shipping weight, 1 pound.

1928 Catalog Page

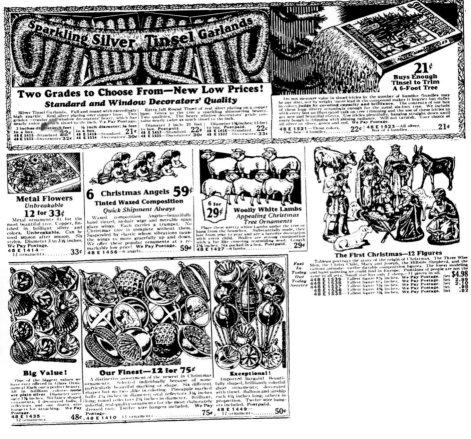

Sparkling Silver Tinsel Garlands

Two Grades to Choose From—New Low Prices!
Standard and Window Decorators' Quality

Silver Tinsel Garlands. Full and round with exceedingly high sparkle. Real silver plating over copper base. Nearly twice as much tinsel to the inch. We Pay Postage.

2 inches diameter, 3 feet in a box.
48 E 1415—Standard..........22¢
48 E 1533—Decorators'32¢

½ inch diameter, 3½ feet in a box.
48 E 1416—Standard..........21¢
48 E 1534—Decorators'........30¢

Extra full Round Tinsel of real silver plating on a copper base. Gives to the tree a sparkling shimmering beauty. Two qualities. The heavy window decorators' grade contains nearly twice as much tinsel to the inch.

Diameter 1 inch, 21 feet to box. Postpaid.
48 E 1517—Standard..........22¢
48 E 1531—Decorators'........30¢

Diameter 1½inches; 15 feet to box. Postpaid.
48 E 1416—Standard..........22¢
48 E 1532—Decorators'........33¢

21¢ Buys Enough Tinsel to Trim A 6-Foot Tree

Do not measure value in tinsel icicles by the number of bundles (bundles may be any size, nor by weight (more lead in the compound makes it heavier but duller in color); judge by covering capacity and brilliance. The contents of one box of these long silvery strands is enough for the usual six-foot tree. We include with every box an illustrated talk on tree trimming and the use of these icicles to set new and beautiful effects. Use icicles plentifully, hanging straight down until every bough is dripping with shining radiance. Will not tarnish. Your choice of all silver or silver, green and red. We Pay Postage.

48 E 1521—Three colors. The box—4 bundles..........22¢
48 E 1523—All silver. Box of 4 bundles..........21¢

Metal Flowers
Unbreakable
12 for 33¢

Metal ornaments fit for the most beautiful tree. Copper, finished in brilliant silver and colors. Unbreakable. Can be used season after season. Six styles. Diameter 3 to 3½ inches. We Pay Postage.
48 E 1414—12 ornaments..........33¢

6 Christmas Angels 59¢
Tinted Waxed Composition
Quick Shipment Always

Waxed composition Angels—beautifully hand tinted; mohair wigs and movable spun glass wings. Each carries a trumpet. No Christmas tree is complete without them. Suspended by elastic which vibrations cause the wings to move gracefully up and down. We offer these popular ornaments at a remarkably low price! We Pay Postage.
48 E 1456—6 angels..........59¢

Woolly White Lambs
6 for 29¢
Appealing Christmas Tree Ornaments

Place these pretty white Lambs under the tree or hang from the branches. Substantially made, they last from year to year and are a favorite decoration with a fur like covering resembling wool. Length 2½ inches. Six packed in a box. Postpaid.
48 E 1427—6 lambs..........29¢

The First Christmas—12 Figures

Tableau portrays the story of the origin of Christmas. The Three Wise Men, the Christ Child, Mary and Joseph, the Hillside Shepherd, and the various animals—twelve durable composition figures. The finest modeling and hand painting we could find in Europe. Positions of people are not the same in all sets. Small size has only 2 sheep—11 pieces in all.

Fast In Today Out Today Service
48 E 1539—Tallest figure 8½ inches. We Pay Postage. Set..........$4.98
48 E 1538—Tallest figure 6½ inches. We Pay Postage. Set..........2.98
48 E 1537—Tallest figure 5½ inches. We Pay Postage. Set..........2.00
48 E 1536—Tallest figure 4½ inches. We Pay Postage. Set...........98
48 E 1535—Tallest figure 3½ inches. We Pay Postage. Set..........82

Big Value!

One of the biggest values we have ever offered in Glass Ornamental Each one a perfect beauty. All in brilliant colors—none are plain silver. Diameter over 1½ inches. Six fancy shaped ornaments, 4 decorated balls, 2 reflectors and one dozen wire hangers for attaching. We Pay Postage.
48 E 1435—12 ornaments..........48¢

Our Finest—12 for 75¢

A distinctive assortment of the newest in Christmas ornaments. Selected individually because of some particularly beautiful marking or shape. Six different shapes but no two alike in coloring. Pineapple shapes 4½ inches long; oval reflectors 3½ inches long; round reflectors 2½ inches in diameter. Twelve high quality ornaments for the most elaborately dressed tree. Twelve wire hangers included. We Pay Postage.
48 E 1410—12 ornaments..........75¢

Exceptional!

Imported bargain! Beautifully shaped, brilliantly colorful glass ornaments; decorated with tinsel. Balloon and airship each 4½ inches long; others in proportion. Twelve wire hangers included. Postpaid.
48 E 1449—12 ornaments..........50¢

1929 Catalog Page

Paper Bells, Wreaths, Balls and Other Decorations

Tissue Paper Bells

N9370—4-in. Tissue Bells. Ht. 4 in., bright red tissue paper, honey comb style, folded and sewed at the edge, enameled cardboard backs with metal clasps to fasten when open. 1 gro. in box. Gro.............

N6567—Red Bell. (Mfrs. 2510.) Ht. 10 in., made of honey-comb tissue with "Merry Christmas Greeting" above bell, printed on both sides and varnished. 3 doz. in box.
Doz........... Gro...........

Hinoki Xmas Bells

Made of Hinoki roping, wrapped over heavy composition board, red body with green hanger and green trimmed bottom.

N8279—3 in., 6 doz. in box.
Doz........... Gro...........

N8280—4 in., 3 doz. in box.
Doz........... Gro...........

N8287—5 in., 1 doz. in box.
Doz........... Gro...........

New Imported Silver Bells

A splendid decorative unit that is certain to add beauty to the home, church or other public place, where a true Christmas atmosphere is desired. Bells are formed in perfect appearance of the real thing from papier mache and covered with silver paper.

N8280S—Bell diam. 4 in., ht. 3 in. Doz., 40c. Gro.............
N8279S—Bell diam. 3 in., ht. 2½ in. Doz., 30c. Gro.............

Jumbo Xmas Bell DECORATION

Makes a fine addition to the decorative scheme

N8630 — Jumbo Bell and Holly Decoration. 15½x18¾ in., printed in bright colors on both sides of cardboard and die-cut with a large 18-inch jumbo bell of red honeycomb tissue. Each with string hanger. Adds to and gives an excellent finish to the display. doz. in box. Doz.,

Xmas Bell and Poinsettia Wreath

N8537 — Silver Poinsettia Wreath and Bell. (Mfrs. 2004.) One design, size 11½x 12 in., printed red and green on silver leaf poinsettias and red Merry Christmas bell, metallic board, embossed and die-cut. 1 doz. in box.

Doz. ....

Gro. ....

Greeting Banners

N9504—Christmas Greeting Decoration. Rustic letters imitation of birch bark, 4½ inches high and 5½ feet long letters die-cut, jointed. 1 doz. in box.
Doz.............. Gro..............

N9512—New Year Greeting Decoration. Rustic letters imitation birch bark, 4½ inches high and 4½ feet long letters die-cut. 1 doz. in box.
Doz.............. Gro..............

Christmas Greeting Sign

Christmas Greeting Banner. Size 1½x15 ft., fine tissue paper, 4 ply, printed red and green, fringe top and bottom, die cut, string reinforcement. Each banner wrapped.
N6569—1 doz. in pkg.. Each............ Doz..............

Decorative Garlands

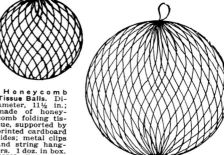

N7820 — Tissue Fringe Garlands. Made of fine red and green tissue paper and holly buttons. With fringe dropping 24 inches and garland extending 10 feet long. Equipped with strings—making decoration ready to hang.
1 Doz. in box. Doz................. Gro.......................

Hinoki Roping

Fine grade, ⅛ in. diam. A popular type of decorating material. Solid colors, green and red, specify colors.
N9378—15 yds. in bdle. Doz bdls..75c
N9378½—8 yds. in bdle. Doz. bdls...40c
N9379—60 yds. in bdle. Bdle.........

Honeycomb Tissue Balls

Honeycomb Tissue Balls. Diameter, 11½ in.; made of honeycomb folding tissue, supported by printed cardboard sides; metal clips and string hangers. 1 doz. in box.
N9505—Red.
N9507—Green.
N9510—Red and Green.
Doz.............. Gro..............
N9511—Red and Green Tissue Ball. Same as above, 1¾ in in diameter. ½ doz. in box. Doz..............

XMAS TREE LIGHTS

S609—Tungsten Loop Set. 8-light, two-tone tungsten bulbs, fancy colored silk cord and 1-piece plug. 1 set in carton.
Set ....
Doz. Sets ....
S610—8-Light Set. Same as above with plug into which another set can be plugged.
Set ....
Doz. Sets ....
N6090 — Noma 8-Light Extension Indoor Set. (Mfrs. 100M). Cotton covered tracer wire, green composition sockets spaced
in. apart. Bakelite tri-plug into which another set can plugged. Eight 15-volt C-6 miniature base assorted lor Mazda lamps. 1 set in box.
t ....
oz. ....

S120— Detector oop Set. Eight mps of assorted lors, 15 volts, e burned-out mp glows, re- ace it and all he lamps will ght up. An ex- ellent value and fast seller.
et ....
oz. Sets.......

S124 — Outdoor Set. Seven lights, 120 volt, water- proof cord sealed in socket to pre- vent short circuit, one-piece plug, assorted color lamps. 1 set in box.
Set ....
Doz. sets......
S125—7-Light Extension Out- door Set. Water- proof colored cord sealed in socket to prevent short circuit, 1-piece plug and exten- sion, 110-volt as- sorted color lamps. 1 set in box.
Set ....

Renewal Lamps for Christmas Tree Sets

N6091—Imported Lamps. ungsten type, 14 volt, 6 c.p., 2- ne color combination. 10 mtd. n card, 100 in carton.
ard of 10 ....
er 100 ....
er 1000 ....
S136—"Staybrite" Imported Lamps. 15-V. Tungsten mps, asstd. colors. When used in tree sets in series of burned out lamps are easily detected as all other lamps series stay lighted. 10 in box.
ox ....
er 100 ....
N6093—Mazda Lamps. 15 volt, 6 c.p., assorted colors, 0 in box.
er 100., $3.65. Box ....
S1351—Imported Detector Lamps. 15 volt, asstd. colors, lament glows when bulb burns out, no time lost in re- lacing defective lamps. 10 in box.
ox ....
er 100 ....
S7052—Outdoor Mazda Lamps. 120-V., (C9½) asstd. olors, intermediate base, 10 in box.
ox ....
er 100 ....
S7053—Outdoor Imported Lamps. 120-V., asstd. colors, ¼ c. p., intermediate base. 10 in box.
ox ....
er 100 ....

Electric Christmas Wreaths

10½ in. wound with red Japanese roping, decorat- ed with silver leaf holly and 3½ in. red bow, metal candle base, 120 v., red bulb, 4½ ft. silk cord.

S6095—1 in box.
Doz. ....

Less than dozen lots. Each............

Xmas Village

Christmas Villages. When used with regular tree light outfits these sprayed houses will give a most colorful effect. Eight houses in a set, opening in back of house large enough to receive 1 bulb, windows have colored transparent panes so that light can show through.
N2525—Average size 3 in.
Per set of 8 ....
N2473—Average size 4½ in.
Per set of 8 ....
N9296—Average size 6 in.
Per set of 8 ....

No. 5921—Christmas Bell. Made of honey- comb Red and Green tissue paper with card- board sides. Printed top as illustrated and string hanger. Height, 10". Two doz.
Per dozen ....
No. 5923—Christmas Bell. Same as above but 13 inches in height. One dozen in box.
Per dozen ....

Tissue Paper Bells, made of honeycomb red tissue paper, in 4 sizes.
No. 5956—4" diam. One gross in box.
Gross ....
No. 5957—6" diam. 6 doz. in box.
Dozen......20¢   Gross......
No. 5958—10" diam. 2 doz. in box.
Dozen......40¢   Gross......
No. 5959—14" diam. One doz. in box.
Dozen......70¢   Gross......

Novelty Indoor Paper Decorations for Christmas

Paper Xmas Trees

Made of honey comb tissue paper. Can be decorated the same as natural trees, with a string of electric lamps, tinsel garlands and glass balls, making a most practical Christmas tree for homes, stores, schools, churches and Sunday School rooms. 26 inches high, 18 inches diam. Folds flat, ½ doz. in box.

N8540—Green tree and red base. Doz..........

N8541—Red tree and green base. Doz..........

Christmas Tree Fences

N8539—Christmas Tree Fence. 6 panels, 12 in. long, 4½ in. high, both sides printed in bright Christmas colors, heavy cardboard, die-cut, with catches so that they can be hooked together to form a fence. 1 set in an envelope. Doz. sets .... Gro..........

Xmas Wreaths

Heavy cardboard bent to half circle and made round, wrapped carefully and closely with Hinoki red roping decorated with spray of evergreen and ribbon bow.

N8827—Diam., 4 in. Doz.......25c Gro.........
N8828—Diam., 6 in. Doz.......40c Gro.........
N8829—Diam., 8 in. Doz.......75c Gro.........
N8834—Diam., 14 in. Doz. ....

Santa Claus Masks

N329—Santa Claus Gauze Mask—Light weight gauze, good forehead, painted features, jute beard and mustache. 3 doz. in box. Doz. ....

N330—Santa Claus Mask. Medium weight gauze, painted features, long white jute beard. Doz..........

N331—Santa Claus Mask —Waxed paper, well painted, jute mustache and beard, red sateen hood. 1 doz. in box. Doz..........

Santa Claus Decorations

N9503—Santa Claus Decoration. Made of red honey comb tissue body, arms and legs, 20 in. high, each with string loop hanger. 3 doz. in box.

Doz..........35c Gro.........
Same as above, with envelopes.
Doz..........40c Gro.........

N9642—Life Size Santa Claus. The newest and most lifelike decoration ever conceived in paper. Stands full 5½ feet high when opened, with a big jolly face that makes every one smile, folds flat for protection and convenience in handling. Packed, tied with tape, each in printed heavy envelope 23x24 inches with directions for setting up.

Each...... Doz.........

Paper Xmas Trees

N8503—Green Fir Tree. (Mfrs. 2083.) Green honeycomb tissue tree with red honeycomb tissue base, printed cardboard sides, wire clips. Size 17x18½ in. 1 doz. in box. Doz. . Gro. .

N8405—Red Fir Tree (Mfrs. 2084.) Same as above, green base and red tree. Doz........ Gro....

Branched Xmas Tree 13½x7½ in., made of honeycomb folding tissue, supported by printed cardboard sides with metal clips. 1 doz. in box.

N2043—Green Tree with red base.
N2044—Red Tree with green base. Doz...... Gro......

Tissue Candle

N8632 — Tissue Candle and Holder. One design, red honey comb tissue candle, holder and candle die-cut in attractive shape, ht. 16½ in., green tissue candle holder size 8½x6½ in. with cardboard sides die-cut with handle, and printed both sides in red. 1 doz. in box. Doz..........65c Gro..........

Xmas Tree Decoration

N9501 — Xmas Tree Decoration. A new novelty Tree Decoration with two small red tissue Bells and a red tissue Ball on the top that opens with a "snap," and supported above a cut-out bird that has designs in colors on both sides. 6 styles. Size 6 in. high by 5 in. spread of wings. Asstd. 6 doz. in box.

Doz. ....
Gro. ....

Xmas Decoration

N9548—Christmas Tree Reflector Sign Decoration. One design, size 15½x12¼ in. An attractive sign printed in colors, decorated with tinsel snow, cut-out greeting letters having silver foil reflector mounted on back to make a showy greeting by reflected night light, as well as an attractive decoration by day. Two honeycomb tissue green fir trees at either side with red base. Each in glassine bag. ¼ doz. in box. Doz....................

Xmas Stockings, Roping, Crepe Paper
and Decorations

No. 5927—Christmas Tissue Ball. Made of honeycomb tissue paper in red and green colors with cardboard sides and metal clips. Opens into beautiful 11½-inch diameter ball. Packed one dozen in box.

Per dozen.............................

No. 5928—Christmas Tissue Ball. Same as above, except 19 inches in diameter, and packed ½ dozen in box.

Per dozen.........................

No. 5900—Red Hinoki Roping. Made of oriental wood fibre in bright red color and is widely used for Christmas decorating. Diameter, 11/16-inch. Put up in 60-yard bolts.

Per bolt.............................
Per dozen bolts.........................

No. 5901—Green Hinoki Roping. Same as above but supplied in bright green color.

Per bolt.............................
Per dozen bolts.........................

No. 5997—Blue Hinoki Roping. Same as above but supplied in rich blue color.

Per bolt.............................
Per dozen bolts.........................

No. 5955—Christmas Tissue Decoration. Consists of red and green colored honeycomb folding tissue top with cardboard sides and metal clips. Tissue fringe hangs from top. An attractive hanging decoration. Size, 11x12 inches. Put up one dozen in box.

Per dozen.............................

No. 5924—Dancing Santa Claus. Head, hands and feet are of lithographed cardboard, legs, arms and body made of red and green meshed tissue paper. Equipped with string hanger. Length outstretched, about 40 inches. Each in cellophane envelope.

Per dozen.........................
Per gross.........................

Unfilled Xmas Stockings. In great demand by churches, clubs, etc., who desire to fill them with articles of their own selection. Made of good quality red netting in three sizes, as listed below.

No. 5913—10 inches long.
Per dozen.............................
Per gross.............................

No. 5914—14 inches long.
Per dozen.............................
Per gross.............................

No. 5915—17 inches long.
Per dozen.............................
Per gross.............................

Filled Xmas Stockings. Each stocking is made of reinforced red netting and is filled with a very fine assortment of attractive toys. Made in two sizes.

No. 5944—14-inch filled with 7 toys.
Per dozen.............................

No. 5945—19-inch filled with 12 toys.
Per dozen.............................

No. 5920—Realistic Christmas Tree. 26 inches high and made of green color meshed tissue paper with red color base. Sturdily made so that it can be trimmed like a natural tree. Packed six in box.

Per dozen.........................

No. 5936 — Realistic Christmas Tree. Same as above except has red color body with green color base.

Per dozen.........................

No. 5917—Christmas Crepe Paper. Excellent quality crepe paper in Christmas colors with brick design. Can be used to make favors or for decorations. Put up in folds 7½ feet long and 20 inches wide.

Per dozen folds.....................

No. 5948 — Christmas Crepe Paper Ribbon. Fine quality crepe paper with fancy bell and holly designs in Christmas colors. Put up in rolls 2½ inches wide and 40 feet long.

Per dozen rolls........

No. 5929—Christmas Crepe Paper. High grade quality crepe paper with fancy holly design. Can be sewed and made up into hats, favors or costumes. Put up in folds 7½ feet long and 20 inches wide.

Per dozen folds...................

1940 Catalog Page

HINOKI ROPING CHRISTMAS WREATHS AND STARS

No. 5939 — Christmas Wreath. Large size heavy cardboard base wrapped very closely with red Hinoki roping. Beautifully decorated with ribbon, evergreen, tinsel stars and silver finish beads. Diameter, 11 inches.

Per dozen............

No. 5964 — Decorated Christmas Star. Designed of red and green Hinoki roping wound on a heavy cardboard base and ornamented with silver colored glass beads and silver finished leaves, with star in center. Diameter, 9 inches. One dozen in box.

Per dozen........................

No. 5938 — Christmas Wreath. Made in large size with heavy cardboard base closely wrapped with red Hinoki roping. Very attractively decorated with tinsel silver finish leaf spray and evergreen with ribbon and pine cone. Diameter. 12 in.

Per dozen...........

No. 5918—Christmas Wreath. Heavy cardboard base closely wrapped with red Hinoki roping. Each wreath decorated with ribbon and spray of evergreen and imitation candle. Diameter, 7 inches.

Per dozen..................

No. 5919—Christmas Wreath. Same as above but 8 inches in diameter.

Per dozen..................

No. 5925—Christmas Wreath. Same as above but 10 inches in diameter.

Per dozen..................

No. 5983—Colored Tinfoil Christmas Wreath. Consists of a cardboard base wrapped with blue tinfoil and decorated with bright silver colored glass beads. Silver and green metallic paper leaves attached at bottom with fancy red color bow. Diameter, 9⅝ inches. One dozen in box.

Per dozen..................

No. 5982—Silver Tinfoil Christmas Wreath. Same as above but wrapped in silver tinfoil with large green glass bead decorations.

Per dozen..................

No. 5906—Christmas Wreath. Made of heavy cardboard and wrapped closely with red Hinoki roping. Decorated with spray of evergreen, pine cone and ribbon. Diameter, 6 inches.

Per dozen..................

No. 5907—Christmas Wreath. Same as above but 8 inches in diameter.

Per dozen..................

No. 5904 — Christmas Wreath. Consists of heavy cardboard closely wrapped with red Hinoki roping. Has ribbon and evergreen decoration and small silver finished bell suspended from top. Diameter, 6 inches.

Per dozen..................

No. 5905—Christmas Wreath. Same as above but 8 inches in diameter.

Per dozen..................

No. 5981 — Silver Tinfoil Christmas Wreath. Handsomely designed of bright silver tinfoil wrapped around a cardboard base and decorated with gold color glass beads. Two silver and blue color metallic paper leaves are attached at bottom with red color bow. A beautiful decoration with instant eye-appeal. Diameter, 9⅝ inches. Packed one dozen in box.

Per dozen..................

No. 5911 — Christmas Wreath. Large size heavy cardboard base closely wrapped with red Hinoki roping. Has small silver finish bell suspended from top and is very attractively decorated with evergreen spray and ribbon. Diameter, 10 inches.

Per dozen..................

No. 5912—Christmas Wreath. Same as above but 12 inches in diameter.

Per dozen..................

1940 Catalog Page

108

Holiday Decorations, Tree Ornaments

NEW ILLUMINATED Tree Top Angel

Magnificent NOMA Decoration

Latest innovation in Xmas tree lighted decoration—a winsome doll-like figure representing the idealistic conception of glorious angelic beings in a halo of light. Attired in a pink or blue garment with golden wings, and in white with silver wings, fitted with C-7½ Mazda Lamp—attached extension cord.

No. T700. Dealer's,
Each,
12, each,
Less 2%, net........

NOMA Silk Candle Wreaths

Complete with 120 Volt MAZDA Bulb

A popular favorite finished in red with antique ivory drip candles and holly spray with poinsettia. AD-ON TRI-PLUG extension for attaching other decorations. 10½ in. diameter. Comes complete with C-7½ 120 volt MAZDA bulb.
No. T261. Dealer's, each,
Lots of 10, each,
Less 2%, net.....................
No. T280. Same as above, but 12 in.
Each,   ea.,   Lots of 10, each,
Less 2%, net.....................

Glorious Electric Lighted CROSS

Finished White with Red Lamps

Finished Red With Red Lamps Specify Color

This beautiful Silk Cross is an ideal religious significant Xmas tree decoration. It stands 11 in. high, is 8 in. wide and as a lighting fixture for the home in the window or on the wall. Choice of white with white lamps or red with red lamps. Complete with 11 C-7½ Mazda lamps. Add-on plug and cord for connecting additional ornaments. LIST PRICE, 1.50.
No. T1200. Specify Red or White.
Each,   Lots of 12,
each,   Less 2%, net.

Brilliant Electric Lighted Decorative Bell Cluster

Silvered-back metallic foil ribbon bow, holly spray decorated, with two C-7½ Mazda lamps in cellorhane bells; cord attached. LIST,
No. TG802. RED; red bells, red lamps.
No. TG803. BLUE; clear bells, blue lamps. Either style, each,
12, each,   Less 2%, net....

Electric Lighted Wreaths

Candle Type

Glazed Green leaves sprinkled with Holly Berries and Red Holly leaves, 3 graduated silver sprayed candles, 20 in. in diameter. Fitted with 120 V. Gen. Mazda Lamps.
No. T1503. Dealer's Price, Each,
2.24.
Lots of 12, each,
2.13.
Less 2%, net.................

No. T1001. Single Candle, similar to the above, with Silver Mistletoe Berries and Glazed Flowered Ornament surrounding the Red Drip Candle, sprayed in Silver. 15 inches in diam. Complete with 120 V. bulb, 2-Way Plug. Dealer's Price, each,
Lots of 12, each,   Less 2%, net.....

Bell Type

Ideal for display anywhere. Lights shine thru the nine bells revealing the words of greeting. Green and red holly, red bells with green letters. Wired and fitted with 9 Mazda C-6 16V lamps in series. Diam. 20 in.
No. T1509. Each,
2.94. Lots of 10,
Ea.,
Less 2%.

Similar to above in garland form. Add-on plug for extra ornaments. Sparkling and colorful. Length 4 feet.
No. T1510. Each, 2.94. Lots of 10, each,   Less 2%, net.............

ADD-ON LIGHT SOCKETS

For Outdoor Light Strings WEATHERPROOF P & S PIN TYPE SOCKET

Attach anywhere on outdoor light-set. Not necessary to strip wires. Contact screws puncture insulation and make contact with wires held rigidly in place by socket cap. Weatherproof construction.
5C464. Edison Base.
Each,   10, Each,
Per 100, Each......................
6C4644. Intermediate Base.
Each,   10, Each,
Per 100, Each......................

Electric CANDOLIERS

No. T197

Distinctive display. Adjustable, Durable Metal Frame with Christmas Scene. Fitted with eight 15 V. Gen. Mazda Colored lamps. 21 in. wide. Comes with silk cord and Two way Plug.
No. T199. Dealer's Wholesale Price. Ea.,   12,
ea.,   Less 2%, net....
No. T197. Drip Candle. 11 in. high. Antique Ivory finish with base to match. Add-on outer Plug-Connector. Complete with 120 V. Genuine Mazda Intermediate Bulb.
Dealer's Price, each,
Lots of 12, each,   Less 2%, net.

NEW HALO-LITE 3-Light Candolier

With Neon-Glow Halos

Clear plastic rings around tips form glowing halos, reflecting light from lighted bulb. Three 2-tone ivory-and-silver finish tall candles on streamline base, with C-7½ orange Mazda lamps. Holly spray trim. Height 18 in. overall. LIST,
No.TR-3140M. Dealer's, Each,
Less 2%, net.....

Cast Iron Xmas Tree Stand

For home use. Cast iron, consisting of three detachable and adjustable legs spread to 15 in. A cup like receptacle holds water. Green enameled finish, fastens on with bolts.
6½ in. High
Takes Trees Up to 2¾ in. Diameter
No. 9593. Dealer's Price, Each,
12, each,
Less 2%, net.

Noma Xmas Tree Base

Sturdy and durable —fits any size tree— illuminated by Eight colored Mazda Lamps — outlets for additional lights. Special water pan, plus pin, plus three screws hold tree straight. Red and Ivory Finish. LIST,
Holds 2 Qts. Water
No. T176. Each,
Lots of 3, each,
Less 2%, net...

NOMA HALOS

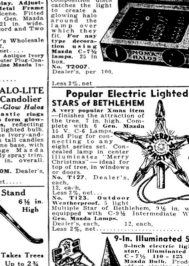

Enchanting new decoration — increases attraction of Xmas lights. Beveled outer edge of the smooth, round transparent composition discs catches the light to create a glowing halo around the lamp over which they will fit. For any type decoration using Mazda C-7½ lamps. 25 in box.
No. T2007. Dealer's, per 100,

Less 2%, net

Popular Electric Lighted STARS of BETHLEHEM

A very popular Xmas item —finishes the attraction of the tree. 7 in. high. Complete with 6 Gen. Mazda 15 V. C-6 Lamps, and Plug for connecting to any eight series set. Concealed lamp in center illuminates "Merry Christmas"—ideal for top of tree, in windows or doors.
No. T127. Dealer's, Each,
12, each,
Less 2%, net....
No. T123. Outdoor Weatherproof, 5 light Multiple Star of Bethlehem, 9½ in. wide, equipped with C-9½ Intermediate White Gen. Mazda Lamps.
Dealer's, each,   12, each,
Less 2%, net...................

9-In. Illuminated Star

9-inch electric lighted star, illuminated by C-7½ 110-125 volt Mazda Bulb. Produces effect similar to Fluorescent lamp. Ideal for hanging in windows or door. Made of sheet metal in white enamel. Specify red, white or blue light. Comes with cord. LIST.
No. T9X. Dealer's, each,
12, each,
Less 2%, net...................

TREE LIGHTS
G. E. Mazda Lamps AMERICAN MADE
NOMA

8-Light SERIES SET

Loop type 8-light series tree light set, with Add-On connector. Complete with 8 assorted color T6 imported lamps. **A Leader Value,** priced below any competition.
No. J39-0.
Lots of 12.

X-L Detector Light Set
Shows Any Burned Out Bulb

8 Light Series Set

As handy as higher priced "independent burning" lamp sets. The bulb that burns out glows, easy to detect, while the others go out. 8 assorted color 15-V. imported Tungsten XL Detector Bulbs on silk cord with colored socket and outlet plug.
No. TX1219.

"TEL-TALE" 8-Light Set

Series Loop Type

Assorted colors Mazda 15-V. Detector lamps. If lights go out, simply press button on each lamp and burned lamp will glow. Has add-on connector.
No. T206. Each, 65c.
12, each, 60c. Less 2%, net.. **59c**

NOMA 8-CANDLE
Set

With Berry Beads

Candle Shape Bulbs 8-Light Series with candle shape 15-volt TC-4½ Mazda lamps in assorted colors. Washers keep lamp tight in sockets, no short circuits. Complete with combination tri-plug for extra sets.
No. 118TC.

MAZDA 15-V. CANDLE LAMPS Mazda Miniature base series candle lamps. 10 of a color to box.
No. C4½. Box of 10

120-Volt INDOOR SETS
Each Lamp Burns Separately
Only Burned Lamp Goes Out

15-LIGHT SET
The deluxe light set for indoor use on larger trees. 15 lights on straight line make tree-trimming easy. Asstd. colors C-7½ 120 V. Mazda lamps, with Berry Bead and Add-on connector.
LIST, 3.00.
No. T3415.

OUTDOOR
Weatherproof 120-Volt
TREE LIGHTS
LEADER 7-Light Set
A well-made set for outdoor use. 7 lights in series on rubber covered wire. Bakelite sockets, with extension connector and plug cap. Complete with seven assorted colored C9½ imported intermediate base Tungsten lamps.
No. TX1806.

NOMA 120-VOLT OUTDOOR LIGHT SETS
7-Light Independent Lamp Set
7-Light Weatherproof Set—has lacquered wire, 13½ in. long, with 3-wire sockets. **Each lamp burns independently.** Fitted with seven asstd. color C9½ inside colored **Mazda lamps,** intermediate Base. Complete with weather-proof cap and connector.
No. T3007.

25-Light, 40 Ft. Straight Line Set
25 Light Multiple Red Cap outfit. Similar to Outdoor Set No. 3007 above. 40 ft. long with 25 assorted color inside frosted C-9½ intermediate base Mazda lamps.
No. T3218.

20 Light Set. Same as T3218 above.
No. T3020.

15 Light Set. Same as T3218 above.
No. T3215.

NOMA NOVELTY SET
Plastic Star and Bell Shapes
Novelty 8-light series outfit with translucent plastic ornaments. Tri-Plug and Add-on connector. Adjustable Berry Beads hold lamps in position on trees. Eight 15-V. C-6 Mazda Lamps, covered with translucent assorted color bells and stars that give unusual effect when lighted on tree. LIST, 1.10.
No. T114.

TREE LIGHT REPLACEMENT BULBS

X-L Detector Lamp, 15-V
To Use with Set TX1219
X-L Patented Bulb "glows" after it is burned out. Easy to locate for replacement if lights go out. 10 of color in box.
No. C116. Pkg of 10, 38c.

120-Volt Mazda Tree Lamp
Independent Burning
Standard candelabra base Mazda 7 watt lamp. For independent-burning sets. 10 of color to box. Assorted colors in box of 100.
No. C7½. Per Box of 10, 52c.

120 Volt 7 Light Set

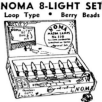

Each lamp burns independently. No more hunting for burned-out lamps. Seven asstd. color 120 V. C7½ candelabra Mazda lamps, with berry beads and Add-on connector.
No. 3010. Each, 98c.

No. T1004. 7-light set, with imported lamps.
12,

NOMA 8-LIGHT SET
Loop Type • Berry Beads

8-Light Series Loop Type. With 15 -V. C6 cone-shaped genuine Mazda Lamps in assorted color beads to hold lamp in position on tree. Tri-Plug connection for adding other sets.
No. T110.

LEADER LIGHT SET. Same as above, less Berry Beads.
No. T108.

NOMA 8-LIGHT SET
Straight Line • Berry Beads
Connection for Added Sets

Outlet Plug
Festoon type 8-light straight line set, with plug-through outlet plug and add-on connector at other end for adding to other strings, for trimming larger trees. Easy to drape on branches. Eight 15-V. C-6 cone type Mazda lamps in assorted colors, with adjustable Berry Beads to hold lamp in position desired.
LIST, 1.10.
No. T100.

REPLACEMENT
15-VOLT BULBS
For Any Series Loop
and Straight Line Set
15-V. MAZDAS
American-made genuine Mazda lamps for use in series-type sets. Extremely popular long-life lamps in most general use. Assorted colors.
No. C-6. Box of 10.

120-V. Intermediate
Base Outdoor
Lamps
Mazda 120-V. Burn independently. Colored inside. 10 asstd. in box. Red, Blue, Green, Orange, and White.
No. C9½.

1941 Catalog Page

CHRISTMAS TREE DECORATIONS

SILVERY RIBBON FOIL ICICLES

Beautiful on Tree

Fireproof icicles that give a beautiful effect to a Christmas tree. 18 inch lead foil strands crimped to give added reflecting surfaces. Packed 2 oz. in non-tangling window carton. Dealer should recommend 6 to 8 boxes for a tree. More and more people are using these icicles alone to decorate their Christmas trees.

No. 285H100—Icicles. Shpg. wt. 4 lbs. List   per box. Net, per dozen boxes (no smaller quantity sold)   Less 2% Net

Net per gross boxes $7.50. Less 2% Net

AMERICAN MADE CORNING FANCY GLASS ORNAMENTS

Dress up the Christmas Tree with these beautiful Corning gleaming molded glass ornaments. Brilliantly finished in an assortment of sparkling new colors. A very attractive item for the dealer—put these on the counter or in the window and watch them go. Each set packed one dozen assorted colors to the box. Size 2¼ inches across. Shipping weight 2 lbs.

No. 276HF214—Fancy Shape Ornaments. Shpg. wt. 2 lbs. List   Net per box of 12 (no smaller quantity sold)   Less 2%
Net
Net per gross   Less 2% Net

GLITTERING SILVER TINSEL GARLANDS

Will Not Tarnish

Glittering silver tinsel that make a tree sparkle. ¾" wide, 9 ft. length in window box. Sparkling fresh, will not tarnish. About 6 boxes needed for tree. These garlands add more sparkle and glitter to a tree than anything else. Fireproof. Used from year to year.

No. 282H2415/6—Garlands. Shpg. wt. 2 lbs. List   per box. Net, per dozen boxes (no smaller quantity sold)   Less 2% Net

Net per gross boxes $8.40. Less 2% Net

STARLIGHT VEIL

Covers Entire Tree With Beautiful Silver Veil

A new distinctive decoration for the Tree. Made of 130 tiny tarnishproof silver strands 6 feet long that spread over the tree like a silver veil. 1 to 4 veils used on average tree.

No. 278H100—Starlight Veil. Shpg. wt. 2 lbs. List   per box. Net each

Net per dozen boxes

AMERICAN MADE CORNING COLORED GLASS ROUND BALLS

Fast selling Corning glass Christmas Tree ornaments in the ever popular round ball shape. Light in weight—just the thing to hang on the ends of branches to give the Christmas tree new sparkling beauty. Packed one dozen to the box in assorted glowing colors of 3 red, 3 blue, 2 green, 2 silver and 2 gold. Size 2⅝ inches across. Shipping weight 2 lbs.

No. 275H258—Round Ball Ornaments. Shpg. wt. 2 lbs. List Net, per box of 12 (NOT BROKEN)   Less 2% Net
Net per gross (144 ornaments)   Less 2% Net

FROSTEE ILLUMINATED SNO BALL REFLECTOR

Adds New Beauty to Lights and Tree

A new and different decoration that fits over Christmas tree lamps. Absolutely fireproof—made of synthetic snow. Hard as frozen snow yet light as a feather. Non-poisonous. Extremely durable—will last for many seasons. An ingenious hidden spring clasp holds Sno Balls firmly to any C6 or C7½ electric tree lamp. Frostee Sno Balls radiate a cheery, colored glow of unusual beauty when illuminated, and reveal a sparkling, crisp snow effect when unlighted. Makes splendid daytime as well as night effect. Packed 8 balls in display box. Two year guarantee on every Sno Ball.

No. 284H—Frostee Sno Balls. Shpg. wt. 1 lb. List   Net per box of 8 (not broken)

AMERICAN MADE UNBREAKABLE CHRISTMAS TREE ORNAMENTS

● Sparkling   ● Brilliant   ● Tarnish-Proof

American made tree ornaments that add brilliance and sparkle to the Christmas tree. Unbreakable feature makes them outstanding sellers. Ornaments are made of substantial pressed paper stock, covered with tarnish-proof lacquered high lustre colored foil. Reflection of tree lights on ornaments produces beautiful scintillating effect. Assorted red, blue, silver, green, and gold colors to the box. Packed 2 dozen of one style (see above) to a box. Boxes not broken. Shpg. wt. 3 lbs.

ROUND BALL

No. 277H590/2—Round Ball. 2½" in diameter. Assorted colors. Per box of 24,   Less 2% Net

TWO-TONE ACORN

No. 280H681/2—Two-Tone Acorn. 2½" long in contrasting colors. Per box of 24,   Less 2% Net

SPEAR PENDANT

No. 279H634/2—Spear Pendant. 5¼" long. Assorted colors. Per box of 24, Less 2% Net

1941-1942 Catalog Page

CHRISTMAS LIGHTING

CANDLE LIGHT XMAS TREES

- **Beautiful Color Effect**
- **Patented Glass Rod Construct.**

Beautiful miniature Christmas trees equipped with brightly shining assorted color candles that never burn out. Ordinary house bulb inside tree lights up the multi-colored candlelights through patented glass rod construction. Eliminates fussing with string of lights. Trees are trimmed in bright luster rayon visca. Are large and full, with sturdy branches in natural effect. Strong and durably constructed. Perfect for home or store decoration.

No. 3051H16/1-Green — 16" Candlelite Tree with 13 Multi-Colored Candlelites. Shipping wt. 6 lbs.

No. 3053H20/1—Green; No. 3050H20/2—White—20" Candlelite Tree with 17 Multi-Colored Candlelights. Shpg. wt. 8 lbs.

No. 3054H27/1—Green 27" Candlelite Tree with 21 Multi-Colored Candlelites. Shpg. wt. 13 lbs.

GLOLITE XMAS TREES

One Bulb Lights Up 17 Miniature Lamps

A novel and different miniature Christmas tree illuminated by one small bulb inside tree. Light from bulb passes up through solid glass rods giving the effect of 17 miniature electrically lighted lamps and star tree top. Not a string of lights that must be constantly replaced. Just plug into light socket to have a beautiful, electric lighted Christmas tree. Complete with lamp, cord, and plug. Glolite trees finished in green or white colored rayon visca. 12" tall.

12" TALL

No. 1330H12/1—Green; No. 1331H12/2—White—Glolite Tree. Shpg. wt. 3 lbs.

NOMA ILLUMINATED 20" HOLLY WREATH

This wreath is radiant with bright, sparkling silvered leaves and clusters of red holly leaves and berries. Constructed on a rigid metal frame and fitted with 9 15-volt T-4 G.E. Mazda red and blue series lamps. Diameter is 20". Complete with 6' of silk-covered wiring and a 2-way connection plug.

No. 654H1508—Noma 20" Illuminated Wreath. (Mfrs. No. 1508). Shpg. wt. 3 lbs.

ILLUMINATED XMAS BELLS

A new and strikingly original adaptation of the ever popular Christmas Bells in a beautiful symbol of Yuletide cheer. Three 5" gleaming cellophane bells, brilliantly illuminated in red, with a red cellophane bow, and silver berries. Each bell equipped with a genuine Mazda lamp. Complete with 3 lamps, cord, and plug.

No. 1325H301 — **Illuminated Christmas Bells.** Shpg. wt. 2 lbs.

ILLUMINATED 12" NOMA HOLLY WREATH

A beautiful low-priced green holly wreath with drip candle and mistletoe decoration at the bottom. Makes a very effective window decoration for home, office, or store. Wreath constructed of closely gathered green leaves with silver color mistletoe berries interwoven to present a very effective contrast. Red drip candle at bottom is sprayed with silver. Complete with one C-7½ 120-volt Mazda lamp, 6' insulated cord, and 2-way connection plug.

No. 653H1502—Noma 12" Green Holly Wreath. (Mfrs. No. 1502). Shpg. wt. 1 lb.

GLOLITE ILLUMINATED ALTAR

- **Realistically Designed** ● **Finished in Marble Effect**
- **With Candles That Will Never Burn Out!**

Realistically designed and finished in marble effect. A 30 watt electric bulb set in the inside of the altar illuminated the 12 candles, the Cross, "The Last Supper," cornices, and chalices. Size: 12" long; 15" high (to top of statue); 5" deep. Altar complete with 30 watt bulb and statue Sacred Heart of Jesus.

No. 1335H206—Glolite Electric Altar. Shpg. wt. 11 lbs.

NOMA ELECTRIC CANDOLIER

- **Simple Classic Design** ● **Smartly Different**
- **With Halo Device**

A beautiful and artistic Candolier with 7 tapered candles equipped with C-7½ Mazda lamps and new halo device which produces a beautiful glow effect. Can be used effectively in windows, as table center piece, on mantel piece, radio, etc. Artistic base: Silver Hollow spray across candles. Candle glow lamps are multiple types, independently burning.

No. 1327H198—Noma 7-Light Candolier. (Mfrs. No. 198). Shpg. wt. 5 lbs.

1941-1942 Catalog Page

NOMA XMAS TREE OUTFITS

DELUXE INDOOR 110 VOLT MULTIPLE LAMP OUTFITS

No More Hunting for Burned Out Lamps.
Each Lamp Burns Independently.

NOMA 3420 OUTFIT

Noma 20-Light Multiple Outfit. New Noma 20-light straight-line set makes large tree trimming easy. Multiple wired with C-7½ candelabra base. 120 volt G.E. Mazda lamps. If one burns out other remain lighted. Easy-sliding berry beads hold lamps upright. Noma Add-on connector for attaching additional sets. Complete with 20 Mazda lamps in assorted colors. **No. 642H3420 — Noma No. 3420 Multiple Indoor Outfit.** Shpg. wt. 3 lbs.

NOMA 3010 OUTFIT

Noma 7-Light Multiple Outfit. Each lamp burns independently—if one goes out, rest of string remain lighted. Has Noma Add-on extension connector for attaching additional sets. Berry beads hold lamps upright. Furnished with washers to keep lamps tight in sockets. With 7 G.E. Mazda 120 volt C-7½ cool burning lamps in assorted colors.
No. 640H3010—Noma No. 3010 Multiple Indoor Outfit. Shpg. wt. 2 lbs.

NOMA 3415 OUTFIT

Noma 15-Light Multiple Outfit. The most popular Christmas lighting set ever made. Straight line design, wired in multiple. Equipped with C-7½ 120 volt candelabra base Mazda lamps. Each lamp burns independently—if one burns out, others remain lighted. The 15 sockets in one straight line make tree trimming a pleasure. With Add-on connector for attaching additional sets and adjustable Berry beads for quick, easy fastening to tree branches. Complete with 15 Mazda lamps in assorted colors.
No. 641H3415—Noma No. 3415 Multiple Indoor Outfit. Shpg. wt. 2 lbs.

NOMA 3425 OUTFIT

No. 643H3425 — Noma No. 3425 Multiple Indoor Outfit. Shpg. wt. 3 lbs. Same as Noma 642H3420 outfit described above, but equipped with 25 G.E. Mazda 120 volt C-7½ lamps in assorted colors.

NOMA OUTDOOR 120 VOLT MULTIPLE OUTFITS

Each Lamp Burns Independently.
Weatherproof Inside Colored Lamps.

NOMA 3005 OUTFIT

Noma 7-Light Outdoor Weatherproof Multiple Outfit. The perfect set for that tree in front of the house. Thoroughly weatherproof. Ideal for indoor or outdoor decorating, particularly where bright illumination is desired. No more frosted fingers searching for that burned out lamp—wired in multiple. Each lamp burns independently. Add-on extension connector for attaching additional sets. Through-wired Red Cap sockets on 13½" length for easy straight-line decorating. Spring contacts keep lamps from getting loose. Complete with 7 G.E. Mazda 120 volt C-9½ lamps, colored on inside for added weather protection. Lamps in assorted colors.
No. 644H3005—Noma No. 3005 Outdoor Weatherproof Multiple Outfit. Shpg. wt. 2 lbs.

NOMA 3020 OUTFIT

Noma 20-Light Outdoor Weatherproof Multiple Outfit. A deluxe set suitable for decorating larger trees, or where more extensive outdoor or indoor installations are required. Same construction as No. 3005 outfit described at left, but with 20 G.E. Mazda 120 volt C-9½ lamps in assorted colors. All lamps inside coated to prevent scratching and fading when used outdoors.
No. 646H3020—Noma No. 3020 Outdoor Weatherproof Multiple Outfit. Shpg. wt. 4 lbs.

NOMA 3215 OUTFIT

No. 645H3215—Noma No. 3215 Outdoor Weatherproof Multiple Outfit. Same as No. 646H3020 outfit above, but with 15 G.E. Mazda 120 volt C-9½ lamps in assorted colors.

NOMA 8-LIGHT SERIES INDOOR XMAS TREE OUTFITS

NOTE: THESE LIGHTS BURN IN SERIES GROUP ONLY—IF ONE GOES OUT, ALL GO OUT.

NOMA 110 OUTFIT

Noma 8-Light Series Loop Outfit. An "eight-in-line" series set that has always been a popular seller. Lamps burn all together—if one goes out, all go out. Tri-plug connector with open outlet for attaching additional sets. May be used with multiple burning outfits. Equipped with 8 G.E. Mazda 15 volt C-6 cone-shaped lamps in assorted colors. For use on 110 volt circuit.
No. 647H110—Noma No. 110 Indoor Series Outfit. Shpg. wt. 2 lbs.

NOMA 140 OUTFIT

Noma DeLuxe 8-Light Series Indoor Straight-Line Outfit. Lamps burn all together as a group only. Add-on connector at both ends for attaching additional outfits and producing continuous string of lights. Has adjustable Berry Beads to hold lamps securely upright on tree branches. Complete with 8 G.E. Mazda 15 volt C-6 lamps in assorted colors. For use on 110 volt circuit.
No. 648H140—Noma No. 140 DeLuxe Festoon Type Series Outfit. Shpg. wt. 2 lbs.

1941-1942 Catalog Page

XMAS NECESSITIES

CHRISTMAS STOCKING

- **Large 29" Size**
- **100% Filled With American Made Toys**

Filled with American made toys. 29 inch Xmas stockings packed in two attractive substantial toy assortments — one for boys and another for girls. Contain games, cutouts, horns, blocks, color books, marbles and a host of other toys. Shipping wt. 3 lbs. each.

— **Boys Stocking. No.** No. 606H10B
607H10G — Girls Stocking.

No. 608HTA8—Combination Boy or Girl Stocking. A smaller stocking filled with toys that will thrill both boys and girls. Shpg. wt. 2 lbs.

GIFT WRAPPING
Complete Assortment
Wraps 30 to 40 Packages

- **31 SHEETS ASSORTED PAPER**
- **100 CARDS, TAGS AND SEALS**
- **30 FT. CELLO RIBBON**
- **42 FT. TINSEL RIBBON**

A big supply of everything required to wrap cheery and attractive Christmas packages. Makes every gift more appreciated.

No. 283H1100—Gift Wrapping Package. Shipping weight 2 lbs.

SANTA CLAUS SUIT

- **Large Size**
- **Tops in Value**

The Christmas season will bring a large and profitable demand for Santa Claus Suits . . . be sure to have a large enough supply, for the rush is sure to come! This complete Santa Suit is good looking and well made throughout; it's a real value at these prices, will satisfy your customers. The suit consists of bright red flannel coat, trousers, and hat trimmed with white; includes white belt, shiny black oilcloth boots and a good Santa mask. Each suit is packed in a separate box.

No. 500H5090—Santa Claus Suit. Large size only.

NOMA ILLUMINATED ALL-METAL CROSS

- **Ideal for Door or Window**

A beautiful illuminated cross that is ideally suited for either door or window. Made of sturdy, attractively finished metal. Measures 10"x7". Light shines through plastic beads for strikingly beautiful effect. Equipped with C-7½ Mazda lamp, extension cord, and plug.

No. 652H1201 — Noma Illuminated All-Metal Cross. (Mfrs. No. 1201). Shpg. wt. 2 lbs.

DECORATIVE MINIATURE TREE ASSORTMENT

- **3 Popular Sizes**   **Fast-Selling**

A fast selling assortment of 21 smooth finish Fibre Christmas Trees in 3 popular sizes. Very suitable for around the home decoration. Can be placed anywhere—under the Xmas tree —table decoration—window sills, etc. Foliage covered with imitation snow giving a very realistic effect—all sizes have red-tub bases—assortment includes twelve trees 1⅝" high, six trees 4¾" high, and three trees 9¾" high. This is a real value. Shipping weight per set 5 lbs.

No. 3056H21—21 Assorted Fibre Xmas Trees. (Assortment not broken.) List per assortment

1941-1942 Catalog Page

Price Guide

Page 4
Top .... 100+
Bottom .... 45+

Page 5
Top .... 35+
BottomLeft .... 75+
Bottom Right .... 50+

Page 6
Top .... 50+
Bottom .... 100+

Page 7
Top .... All 50+
Bottom .... All 150+

Page 8
Top Right .... 100+
Top Left .... 125+
Bottom .... 60+

Page 9
Top .... 50+
Bottom .... 50+

Page 10
Top Left .... 35+
Top Right .... 90+
Bottom .... 40+

Page 11
Top Left .... 60+
Top Right .... 40+
Bottom Left .... 150+
Bottom Right .... 50+

Page 12
Top Left .... 150+
Top Right .... 100+
Bottom Left .... 75+
Bottom Right .... 100+

Page 13
Top Left .... 175+
Top Right .... 150+
Middle .... 40+
Bottom .... 50+

Page 14
Top .... 45+
Middle Left .... 20+
Middle Right .... 50+
Bottom .... 40+

Page 15
Top .... 45+
Top Middle .... 25+
Top Right .... 50+
Bottom Left .... 50+
Bottom Right .... 30+

Page 16
Top Left .... 150+
Top Right .... 100+
Bottom Left .... 200+
Bottom Right .... 200+

Page 17
Top .... 10+
Bottom .... 10+

Page 18
Top .... 30+
Bottom Left .... 50+
Bottom Middle .... 35+
Bottom Right 45-50

Page 19
Santa with Ashtray .... 40+

Page 20
Top Left .... 40+(Set)
Top Right .... 35+(Set)
Middle Right .... 25+(Set)
Bottom Left .... 15+
Bottom Right .... 100+

Page 21
Top Left .... 15+
Top Right .... 30+
Bottom Left .... 10+
Bottom Middle .... 20+
Bottom Right .... 10+

Page 22
Top Left .... 40+
Top Right .... 40+

Page 23
Top Left .... 20+
Top Middle .... 15+
Top Right .... 25+
Bottom Left .... 15+
Bottom Right .... 25+

Page 24
Top Left .... 40+
Top Right .... 45+
Middle .... 150+
Bottom Left .... 50+
Bottom Right .... 25+

Page 25
Top Left .... 25+
Top Middle .... 15+
Top Right .... 45+
Bottom Left .... 75+
Bottom Right .... 200+

Page 26
Top .... 30+
Middle Left .... 20+
Middle Right .... 20+
Bottom .... 25+

Page 27
Top .... 15+
Middle .... 15+
Bottom .... 15+

Page 28
Top Left .... 40+
Top Right .... 30+
Bottom Left .... 25+
Bottom Right .... 35+

Page 29
Top Left .... 25+
Top Right .... 30+
Bottom Left .... 60+
Bottom Right .... 40+

Page 30
Top Left .... 60+
Top Right .... 75+

Bottom Left .... 60+
Bottom Middle .... 40+
Bottom Right .... 75+

Page 31
Top Left .... 25+
Top Right .... 30+
Bottom .... 20+

Page 32
Top Left .... 15+
Top Middle .... 20+
Top Right .... 15+
Bottom Left .... 15+
Bottom Middle .... 15+
Bottom Right .... 15+

Page 33
Top .... 200+
BottomSanta .... 30+
Bottom Misc. .... 10+

Page 34
Top Left .... 10+
Top Right .... 20+
Bottom Left .... 15+
Bottom Right .... 15+

Page 35
Top .... 20+
Bottom Left .... 20+
Bottom Right .... 15+

Page 36
Top Left .... 35+
Top Right .... 10+
Bottom Left .... 20+
Bottom Middle .... 15+
Bottom Right .... 20+

Page 37
All .... 2-4 Each

Page 38
All .... 2-4 Each

Page 39
Top Left .... 75+
Top Right .... 30+
Bottom .... 40+

Page 40
Top Left .... 10+

Top Right .... 15+
Bottom Left .... 2-4+
Bottom Right .... 15+

Page 41
Top:
 Snowman 40-50
 Santas 25-40
Middle Left .... 15+
Middle .... 80+
Middle Right .... 15+
Bottom
 Bird .... 10+
 Boy .... 10+
 Lanterns .... 5+
 Houses .... 15+

Page 42
Top Left 10-15
Top Right .... 25+
Bottom .... 15+

Page 43
All .... 20+ (Set)

Page 44
All .... 25+ (Set)

Page 45
Cardboard Santa .... 100+

Page 46
Top .... 90+
Bottom .... 10+

Page 47
Top 40
Bottom 75

Page 48
Top Left .... 35+
Top Right 225
Bottom 500

Page 49
Top Left 200-250
Top Right 200
Bottom Left .... 60+
Bottom Right 25

Page 50
Top .... 15+
Bottom Left 225

Bottom Right 100

Page 51
Page .... 100+

Page 52
Top 100
Bottom Left .... 115+
Bottom Right .... 250+

Page 53
Cardboard Santa .... 50+

Page 54
Top 250
Bottom 75

Page 55
Top Left .... 25+
Top Right .... 50+
Bottom Left .... 50+
Bottom Right .... 50+

Page 56
Top Left .... 35+
Top Right .... 50+
Bottom Left .... 45+
Bottom Right .... 10+

Page 57
Top .... 15+
Bottom .... 35+

Page 58
Top Left .... 35+
Top Right .... 35+
Bottom .... 35+

Pages 59-73
Prices are located on the page.

Page 74
Page .... 60+

Page 75
Top .... 60+
Bottom .... 25+

Page 76
Top .... 65+
Bottom .... 40+

Page 77
Top .... 25+
Bottom .... 30+

Page 78
Top 50
Bottom .... 225 (Set)
Page 79
Top Left 225
Top Right 75
Bottom 50
Page 80
Top 100
Bottom .... 50+
Page 81
Top Left 65
Top Right 50
Bottom Left 50
Bottom Right 50
Page 82
Top 50
Bottom Left 100
Bottom Right 100
Page 83
Top 225
Bottom 75
Page 84
Top Left 2,500
Top Right 250
Bottom 75
Page 85
Top 200
Middle.................................. 165
Bottom 45-50
Page 85
Top .... 60+
Bottom .... 25+
Page 86
Top Left 175
Top Right 200
Bottom Left 125
Bottom Right 175
Page 87
Top Left 175
Top Right 175
Bottom Left 235

Bottom Right 175
Page 88
Top 175
Middle.................................. 185
Bottom 45-50
Page 89
Top Left 185
Top Right 225
Bottom Left 195
Botton Right 200
Page 90
Top Left 150
Top Right 100
Bottom 100
Page 91
Postcard 75-90
Page 93
Tree Asst. .... 1000+
Orn. Box 12 .... 240+
Mask .... 100+
Tree Candy Boxes .... 75+
Stocking .... 250+
Toy Tree .... 25+
Page 94
Tree Orn. .... 200+ (Per Box)
Tinsel Glass Orn. .... 20+
Stockings .... 200+
Snow .... 25+
Lighting Outfit .... 100+
Candle Holders 5-10
Kringlets .... 100+(A Box)
Page 95
Orn. Top Row .... 40+
Glass Balls .... 25+
Birds ....15+ (Each)
Bells .... 8+ (Each)
Angel .... 40+
Beads .... 10+
Fruit Orn. .... 25+
Metal Foil Orn. .... 15+
Page 96
Top Left .... 500+
Top Right .... 500+
Mask + Hood .... 25+

Mask and Robe .... 75+
Lighting Outfits .... 35+
Trees .... 200+
Bottom Row 20-30

Page 97
Figures First Group .... 75+
Second Group .... 50+
Third Group .... 50+

Page 98
Figures 35-100
Boxes .... 60+
Music Box .... 150+

Page 99
Original Mint Condition
Large .... 500+
Small .... 300+

Page 100
Original Mint Condition ..... 500+

Page 101
#420 .... 125+
#1000 .... 30+
#1500 .... 25+
Fancy Lamps .... 25-50 (Each)
Plain Lamps 10 Box .... 20+
Tree Holder .... 10+

Page 102
Page .... 100+

Page 103
Tinsel Garlands in Box 10-15
Icicles in Box 10-15
Metal Flowers .... 50+ (A Box)
Angels .... 75+ (A Box)
Lambs .... 50+ (A Box)
The Christ. Figures 50-75(A Box)
Orn. Bottom Left . . .40+ (A Box)
Bottom Middle .... 75+ (A Box)
BottomRight .... 60+ (A Box)

Page 104
All on Page .... 15+

Page 105
Lites Set .... 35+
Wreath .... 25+
Village .... 50+

Bells .... 10+

Page 106
All On Page 10-25

Page 107
All on Page 5-10

Page 108
All on Page .... 25+

Page 109
All on Page 15-25

Page 110
All Sets on Page 10-20
Except
    #118TC 25-35
    #T114 25-35

Page 111
Ornaments Box of 12 .... 60+
Box of 24 .... 120+
Sno-Balls .... 5+ (Each)
Icicles, Garland, Etc. 7-10

Page 112
Candelholder 15-25
Candle Lite Tree 25-50
Glolite Tree 15-25
Altar 30-50
Others 10-20

Page 113
All on Page 20-30

Page 114
Stocking .... 100+
Santa Suit 75-100
Cross 20-30
Tree Asst. Set of 3 15-25